MAKE YOUR OWN
RIDING CLOTHES

MAKE YOUR OWN RIDING CLOTHES

JEAN PERRY

illustrated by
WILLIAM PERRY

J. A. ALLEN
London

By the same author
Make Your Own Horse Equipment
Make Your Own Horse Clothing

Published in Great Britain in 1998 by
J. A. Allen & Company Limited
1 Lower Grosvenor Place, Buckingham Palace Road,
London SW1W 0EL

© Jean Perry, 1998

British Library cataloguing-in-publication data
A catalogue record for this book is available from the British Library.

ISBN 0–85131–718–9

No part of this publication may be
reproduced, stored in a retrieval
system, or transmitted, in any form
or by any means, electronic, mechanical,
photocopying, recording, or otherwise,
without the prior permission, in writing,
of the publishers.

Printed in Great Britain by
Hillman Printers (Frome) Ltd, Frome, Somerset

Contents

	Page
Introduction	1
To neaten seams	2
Stock (1)	4
Stock (2)	7
Quilted waistcoat (1)	10
Quilted waistcoat (2)	13
Quilted jacket	17
Hunting waistcoat	23
Jodhpur pattern (a pattern conversion)	29
Jodhpurs	32
Breeches pattern (a pattern conversion)	36
Breeches	39
Show/hacking jacket pattern (a pattern adaptation)	43
Show/hacking jacket (to make)	53
Crash hat cover with six segments	59
Crash hat cover – other designs	64
Racing silk	67
Chaps	74
Culottes	78
Soft leather hat	84
Hooded rain cape	89
Driving apron	94
Side-saddle habit	98

Acknowledgements

I would like to extend my thanks to Christine Alers-Hankey, Allyson Barnes, Anne Cross and Edna Harding for their help in the writing of this book.

Introduction

This third *Make Your Own ...* book is again aimed at those who like the satisfaction of doing things for themselves.

The items range from a simple stock, which can be tackled by anyone, through those which will need to be made by someone who is already a reasonably competent dressmaker, to a show jacket and a side-saddle habit which need tailoring skills.

No special paper is required for making patterns – newspaper (with the sheets stuck together with sellotape) is quite adequate if you only intend to use the pattern once or twice, for both converting the graph patterns to full size and for adapting or converting ready-made commercial patterns. Use a thick black felt-tipped pen to draw gridlines on newspaper. If you intend to use it several times, strong brown wrapping paper is more suitable for the finished pattern.

A back protector has not been included. Although it would be relatively easy to make, such an important safety item should comply to the relevant British or European standard.

It is a good idea to make up a rough garment from old sheeting or cheap cotton to make sure of fit and other adjustments before cutting into expensive material, especially for the complicated shape of the side-saddle skirt/apron.

All measurements are given in both metric and imperial units.

Each pattern states whether or not a seam allowance has been included. If it is included it is always 1.25 cm ($^1/_2$ in).

When taking chest/bust and hip measurements, 5 cm (2 in) should be added to allow for movement unless otherwise stated.

To neaten seams

The following methods are quick and easy and can be applied to flat seams and those pressed to one side, but you could use any other method you prefer. There is no need to neaten seams which are enclosed in lining.

1. Zigzag machine stitch along each of the raw edges of the seam (Fig. 1).

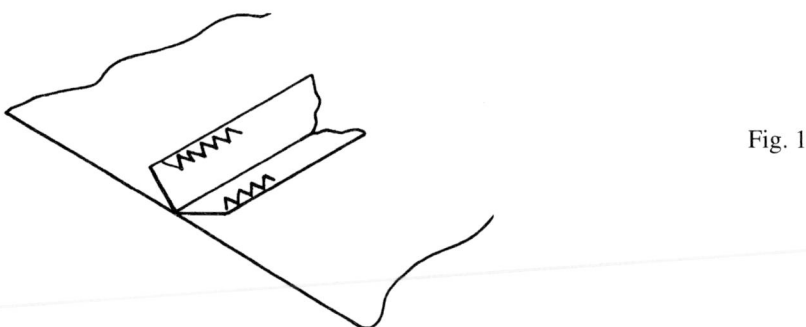

Fig. 1

2. Fold the raw edges under and zigzag machine stitch along the folded edge (Fig. 2).

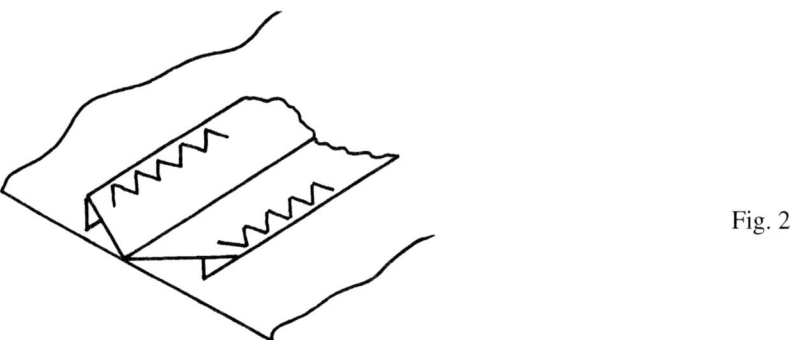

Fig. 2

3. Fold the raw edges under and straight machine stitch along the folded edge (Fig. 3).

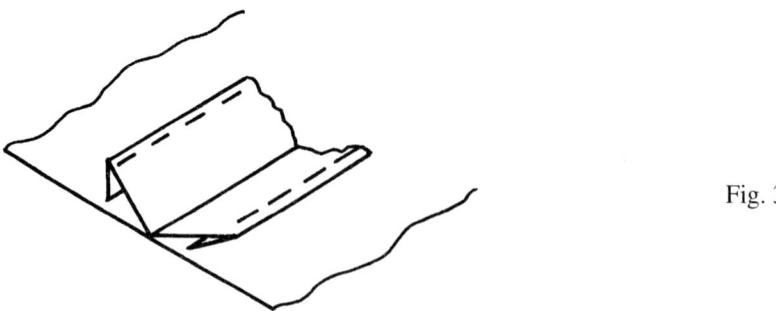

Fig. 3

4. Bind the raw edges with bias binding as follows:

   (a) Unfold one edge of the bias binding, and straight machine stitch this to the underside of the seam (Fig. 4).

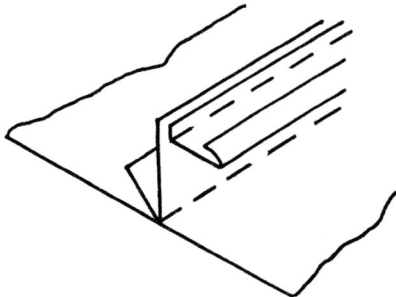

Fig. 4

   (b) Wrap the binding around the raw edge of the seam and straight machine stitch along the folded edge of the bias binding (Fig. 5).

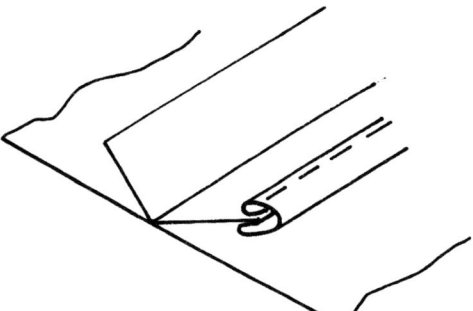

Fig. 5

Stock (1)

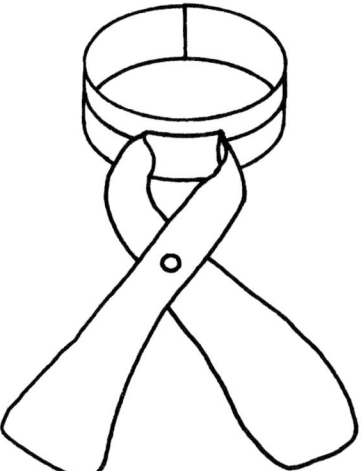

You will need

A piece of soft white cotton material 114 cm (45 in) by 30 cm (12 in).

Sewing thread.

To make

1. Cut out one pair of piece A and one pair of piece B.

2. Working on piece A, place right sides together and join together around the three sides shown in Fig. 6

Fig. 6

3. Cut off the corners of the seams as shown in Fig. 7.

Pattern A   stock (1)

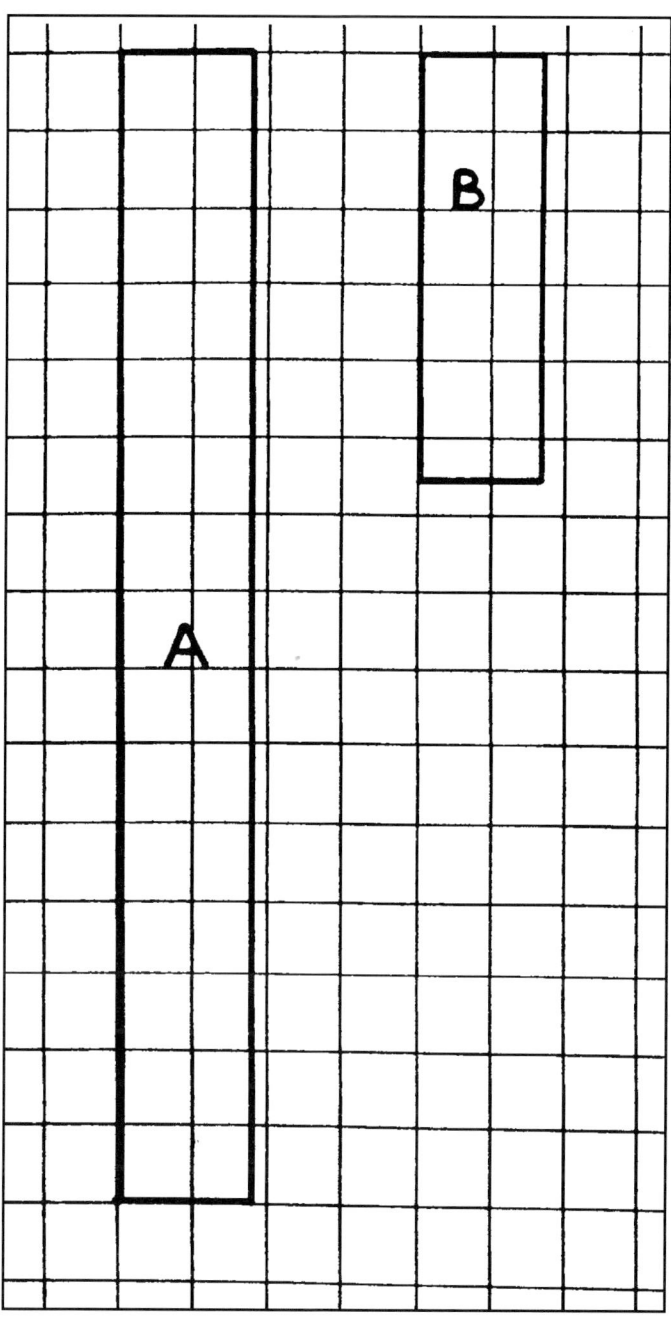

Each square represents 7.5 cm (3 in).

A seam allowance of 1.25 cm ($^1/_2$ in) has been allowed all round.

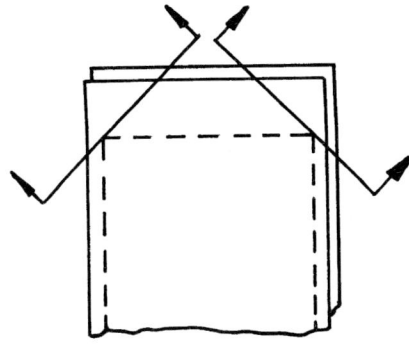

Fig. 7

4. Turn through to the right side and press.

5. Fold in the raw edges, run a gathering thread to reduce the width to 5 cm (2 in) and machine stitch across the end (Fig. 8).

Fig. 8

6. Repeat with piece B.

7. Place the two top-stitched gathered edges together and join with loose hand stitches. Make one or two buttonhole stitches over these (Fig. 9).

Fig. 9

Stock (2)

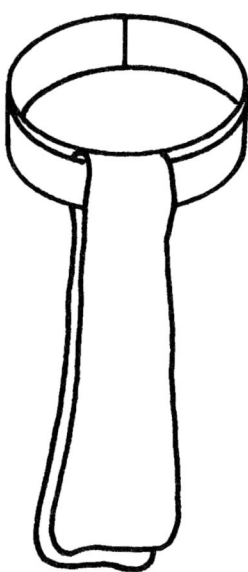

You will need

A piece of crisp white cotton material 102 cm (40 in) by 25 cm (10 in).

Sewing thread.

To make

1. Cut out one pair of piece A and one pair of piece B.

2. Working on piece A, place right sides together and join together around the three sides shown in Fig. 10.

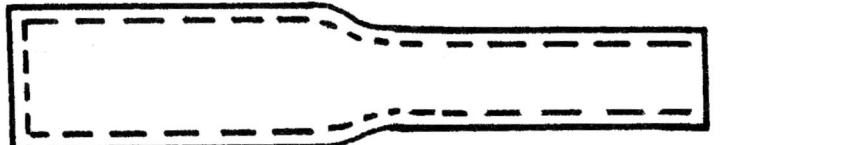

Fig. 10

3. Cut off the corners of the seams as shown in Fig. 11.

Pattern B   stock (2)

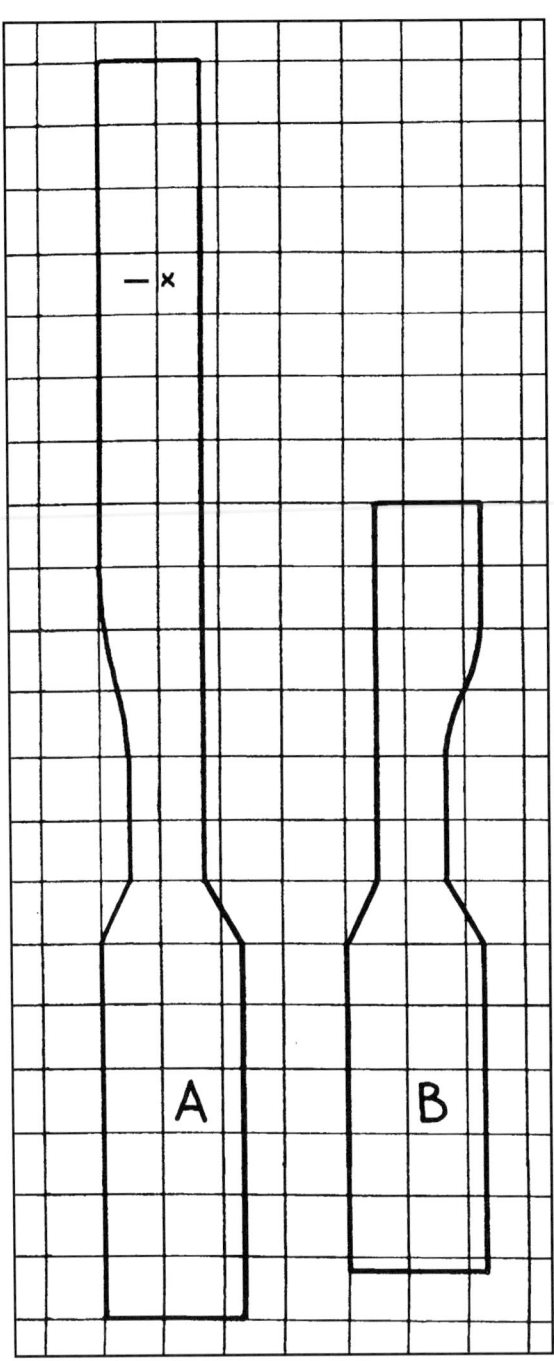

Each square represents 5 cm (2 in).

A seam allowance of 1.25 cm ($^1/_2$ in) has been allowed all round.

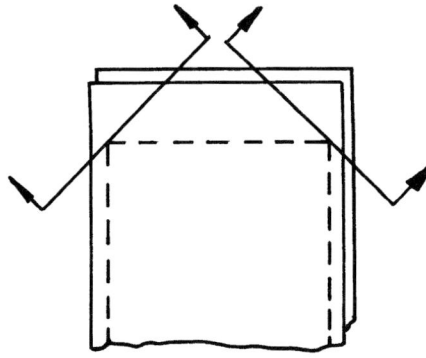

Fig. 11

4. Turn through to the right side and press.

5. Fold in the raw edges and machine stitch across the end (Fig. 12).

Fig. 12

6. Repeat with piece B.

7. Place the two top-stitched edges together and join with loose hand stitches. Make one or two buttonhole stitches over these (Fig. 13).

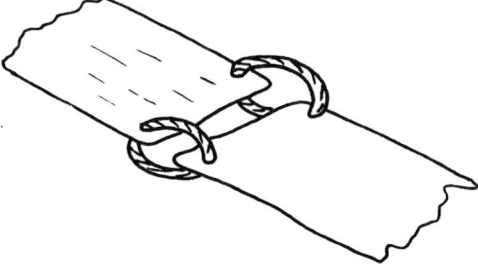

Fig. 13

8. Make a buttonhole at the point marked X on the pattern. When worn, the stock is attached to the front neck button of the shirt.

Quilted waistcoat (1)

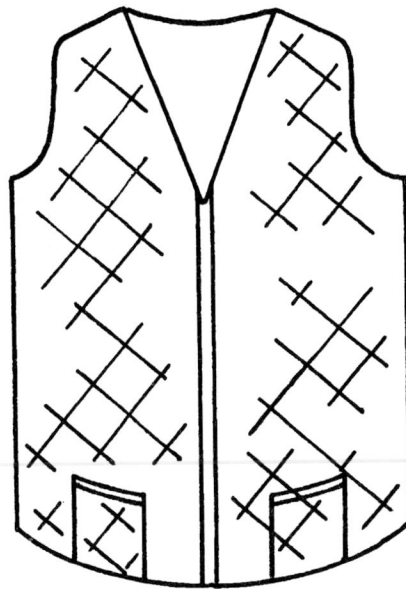

First take the following measurements:

a) chest or bust measurement over the type of clothing you would wear with this garment;

b) the distance from the neck edge of your shoulder seam to the lower hem of the finished waistcoat.

You will need

A sewing machine capable of zigzagging if you are going to neaten the seams this way.

150 cm (50 or 60 in) wide quilted fabric the length of the finished waistcoat plus 2.5 cm (1 in). There will be enough left over for cutting the pockets.

An open-ended zip long enough to fit the front opening.

Scissors.

Sewing thread.

Optional bias binding for seam neatening.

Pattern C quilted waistcoat (1)

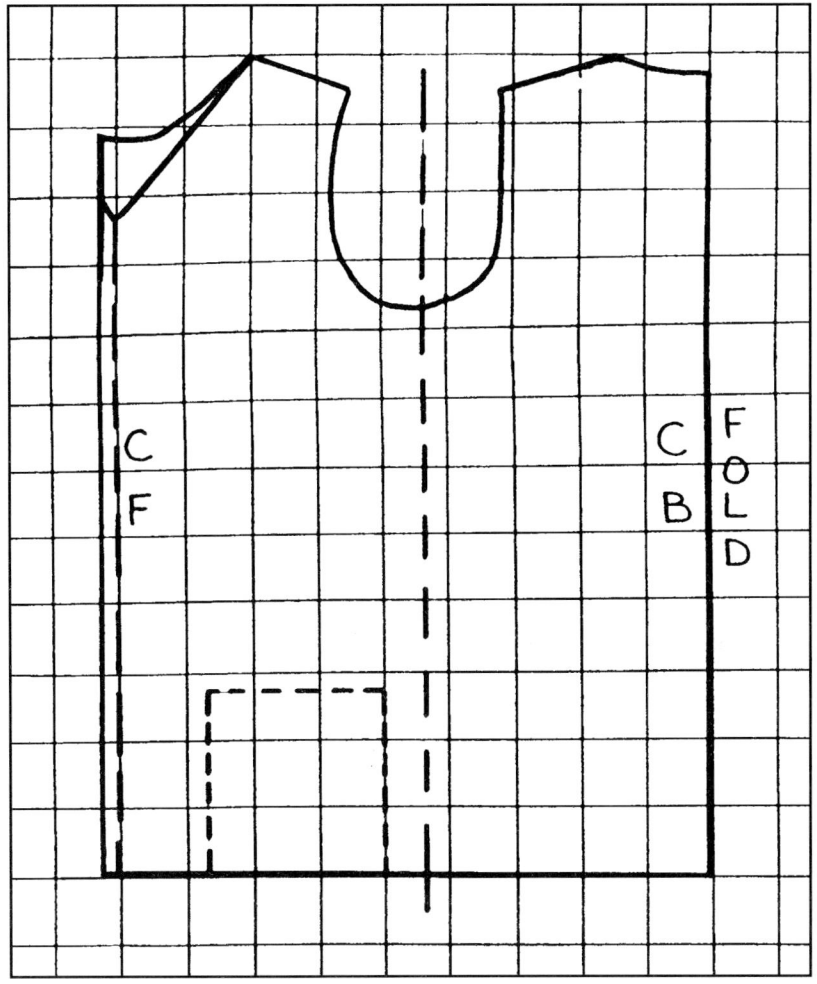

Divide finished length by 12 to find the height of each row.

Divide half the chest or bust measurement by 9 to find the width of each column.

Add 1.25 cm ($^1/_2$ in) all around to finished pattern for seam and hem allowance, including pockets.

Cut around solid lines only for body – choose a round or V-neck.

Cut out two pockets indicated by broken lines.

To make

1. Cut out one main piece and two pockets according to the pattern.

2. Join the shoulder seams, neaten and press flat.

3. Neaten the edges of the neck, armholes, front edge and lower hem.

4. Turn in a 1.25 cm ($^1/_2$ in) hem all round the neck, armholes and lower hem and machine stitch in place.

5. Fold in 1.25 cm ($^1/_2$ in) along both front edges and insert the zip (as it is open-ended it can be inserted as two separate pieces. (Fig. 14)

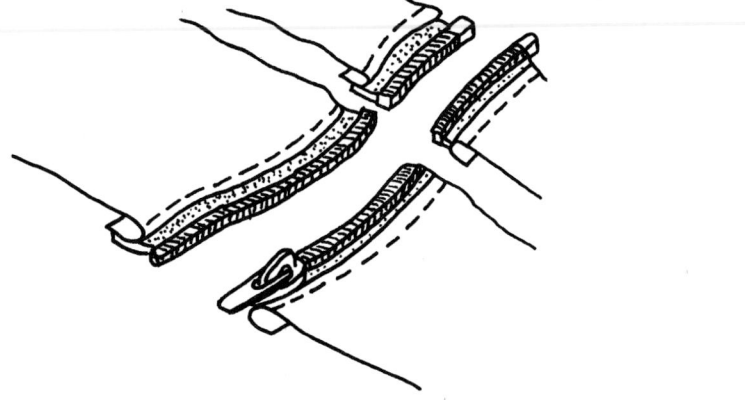

Fig. 14

6. Neaten all around the edges of the pockets.

7. Identify the top of the pocket and make a 1.25 cm ($^1/_2$ in) hem.

8. Fold under 1.25 cm ($^1/_2$ in) around the remaining three sides of the pocket and tack into position on the waistcoat before machine stitching in place.

Quilted waistcoat (2)

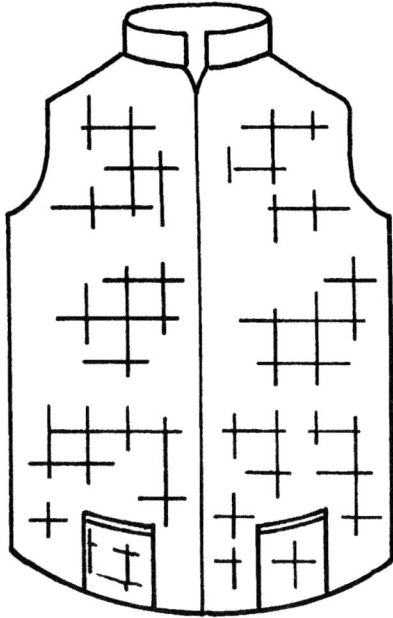

First take the following measurements:

a) chest or bust measurement over the type of clothing you would wear with this garment;

b) the distance from the neck edge of your shoulder seam to the lower hem of the finished waistcoat.

You will need

A sewing machine capable of zigzagging if you are going to neaten seams this way.

150 cm (50 or 60 in) wide quilted fabric the length of the finished waistcoat plus 2.5 cm (1 in). There will be enough left over for cutting the facings, pockets and collar.

An open-ended zip long enough to fit the front opening.

Scissors.

Sewing thread.

Optional bias binding for seam neatening.

Pattern D   quilted waistcoat (2)

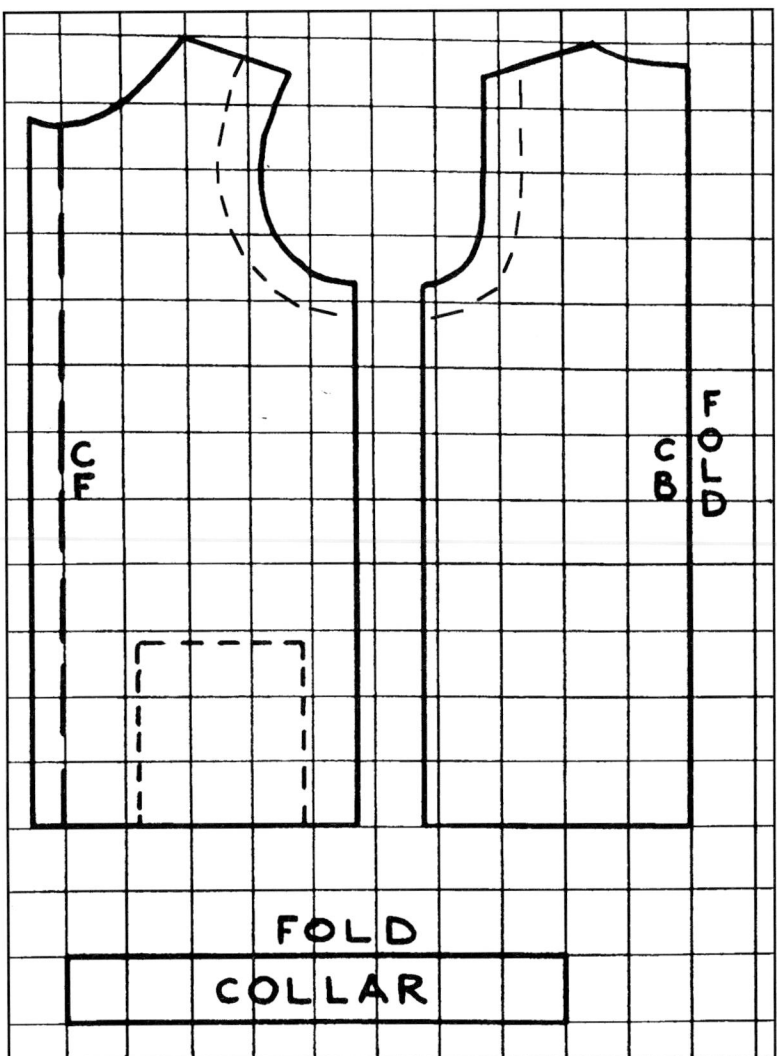

Divide finished length by 12 to find the height of each row.

Divide half the chest or bust measurement by 9 to find the width of each column.

Add 1.25 cm ($^1/_2$ in) all around to finished pattern for seam and hem allowance, including pockets and collar.

Cut around solid lines only for body.

Cut out two pockets and two pairs of armhole facings indicated by broken lines.

To make

1. Cut out one back, two fronts, one collar, two pockets and two pairs of armhole facings according to the pattern.

2. Join and neaten the shoulder seams and press flat.

3. Fold the collar in half, right sides together and join across the two short ends, leaving 1.25 cm ($^1/_2$ in) unstitched at the raw edges and curving the stitching at the folded edge. (Fig. 15) Trim away the material around the edge of the curve. Turn through to the right side.

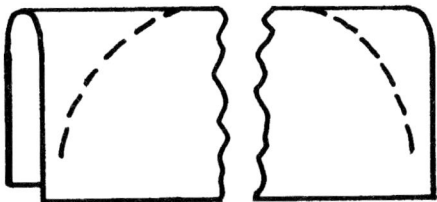

Fig. 15

4. Neaten the front edges of the waistcoat, turn them in by 1.25 cm ($^1/_2$ in) and tack in place.

5. Place one long edge of the collar along the right side of the neck edge and stitch in place (Fig. 16).

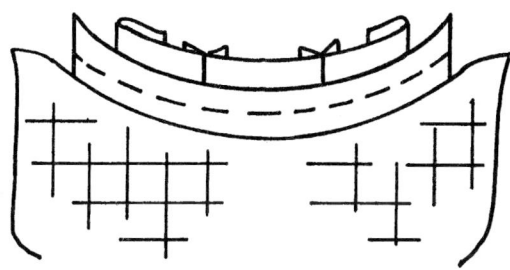

Fig. 16

6. Snip along the seam (Fig. 17).

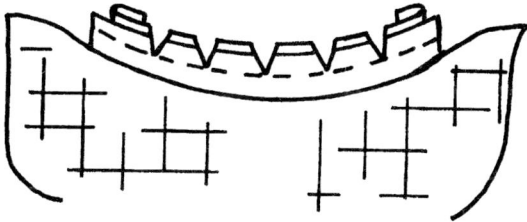

Fig. 17

7. Stitch the other long edge of the collar in place so that it encloses the neck and collar raw edges. (Fig. 18)

Fig. 18

8. Join the side seams.

9. Join and neaten the shoulder and underarm seams of the two armhole facing pieces. Neaten the outer edges.

10. Place the right sides of the armhole facings to the right sides of the armholes and stitch in place.

11. Turn in a 1.25 cm ($^1/_2$ in) hem all round the lower hem and machine stitch in place.

12. Insert the zip (as it is open-ended it can be inserted as two separate pieces). Remove the tacking stitches (Fig. 19).

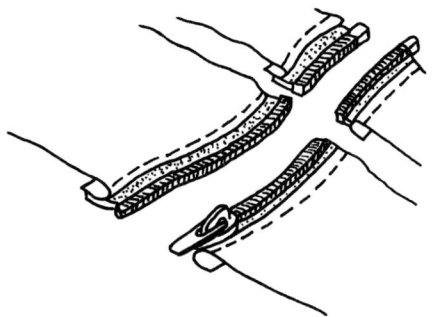

Fig. 19

13. Neaten all around the edges of the pockets.

14. Identify the top of the pocket and make a 1.25 cm ($^1/_2$ in) hem.

15. Fold under 1.25 cm ($^1/_2$ in) around the remaining three sides of the pocket and tack into position on the waistcoat before machine stitching in place.

Quilted jacket

First take the following measurements:

a) chest or bust measurement over the type of clothing you would wear with this garment;

b) the distance from the neck edge of your shoulder seam to the lower hem of the finished jacket;

c) the length of your arm from shoulder to wrist taken while your forearm is folded across your waist.

You will need

A sewing machine capable of zigzagging if you are going to neaten seams this way.

150 cm (50 or 60 in) wide quilted fabric the length of the finished jacket plus the length of the sleeves plus 5 cm (2 in). (There will be enough left over for cutting the pockets, neck facing and collar.)

Heavy grade press studs for front and side vent fastenings.

Scissors.

Sewing thread.

Optional bias binding for seam neatening.

Pattern E   quilted jacket body

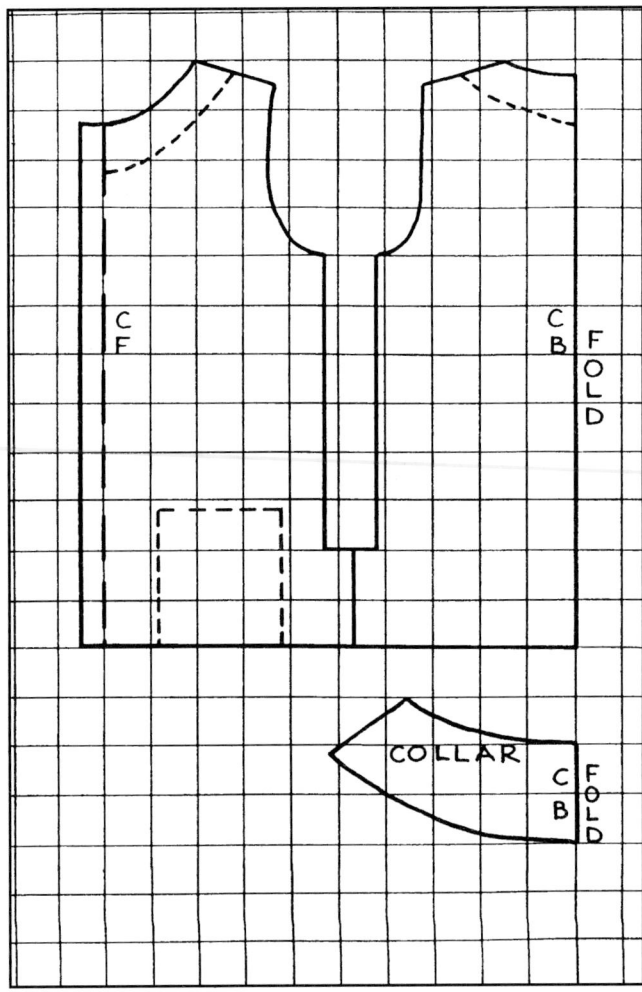

Divide finished length by 12 to find the height of each row.

Divide the chest or bust measurement by 9 to find the width of each column.

Add 1.25 cm ($^1/_2$ in) all around to finished pattern for seam including pockets and collar and 2.5 cm (1 in) for hem.

Cut around solid lines only for body.

Cut out one back neck facing, two front neck facings and two pockets indicated by the broken lines.

Pattern F   quilted jacket sleeve

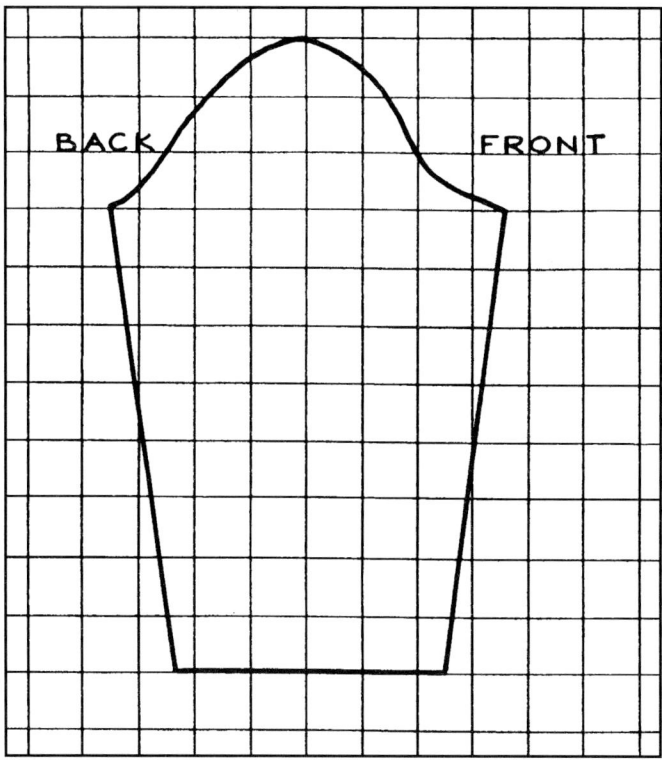

Divide finished length by 11 to find the height of each row.

Divide distance round upper arm plus 5 cm (2 in) by 7 to find the width of each column.

Add 1.25 cm ($^1/_2$ in) all around to finished pattern for seam allowance and 2.5 cm (1 in) for hem.

Cut around solid lines only.

To make

1. Cut out one back and a pair of front pieces, two sleeves, one pair of collar pieces, one back neck facing, two front neck facings and two pockets according to the pattern.

2. Join and neaten the shoulder seams and press flat.

3. Join the collar pieces, right sides together as shown in Fig. 20.

Fig. 20

4. Snip of the corners and turn the collar right side out. Press.

5. Join the front and back neck facings at the shoulder and neaten the outer curve only (Fig. 21).

Fig. 21

6. Place and pin the collar between the body of the jacket and the neck facing and machine stitch in place (Fig. 22)

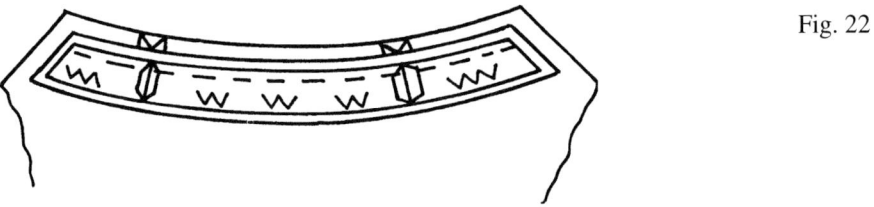

Fig. 22

7. Ease the top of the sleeve into the armhole, and stitch.

8. Zigzag both layers of the armhole seam together to neaten.

9. Neaten and make a 2.5 cm (1 in) hem along the bottom edges of the back, front and sleeves.

10. Join the sleeve seams and side seams down to the vent in one run.

11. Snip into the seam at the top of the vent on the back and fold in half of the vent allowance. Stitch in place (Fig. 23).

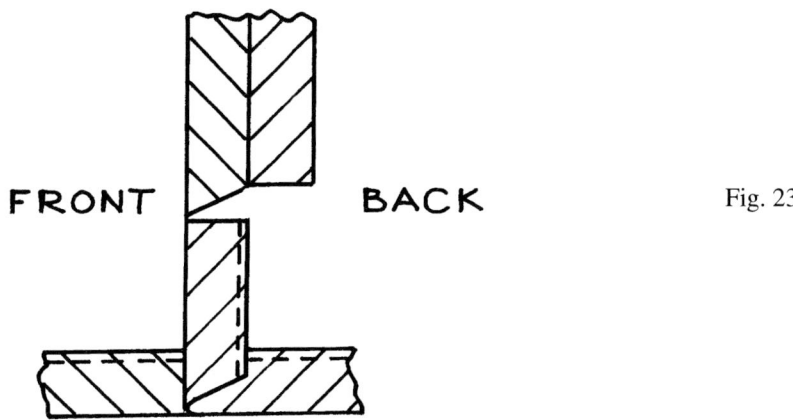

Fig. 23

12. Fold in the whole of the vent allowance on the front and stitch in place (Fig. 24)

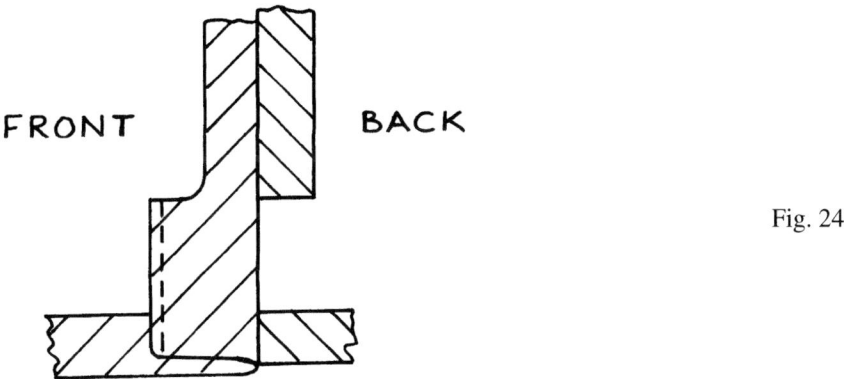

Fig. 24

13. Stitch across the top of the side vent (Fig. 25).

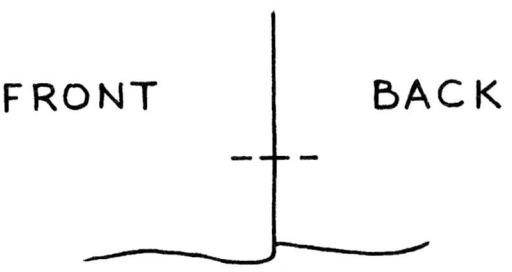

Fig. 25

14. Stitch all around the edge of the collar 1.25 cm ($^1/_2$ in) from the edge.

15. Stitch along the join where the collar meets the body to hold the collar and facing flat.

16. Neaten all around the edges of the pockets.

17. Identify the top of the pocket and make a 1.25 cm ($^1/_2$ in) hem.

18. Fold under 1.25 cm ($^1/_2$ in) around the remaining three sides of the pocket and tack into position on the jacket before machine stitching in place.

19. Add heavy duty press studs to the front edges and the side vents.

Hunting waistcoat

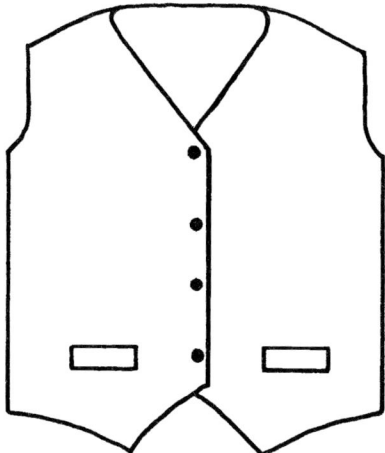

First take the following measurements:

a) chest or bust measurement;

b) the distance from the back neck edge of your shoulder to the back of your waist.

You will need

Sufficient checked or plain yellow or white material for the two halves of the front.

Sufficient lining material for the two halves of the front and two complete backs.

Interfacing for pocket tops.

For a crisp finish, iron-on interfacing for the two halves of the front.

Buttons.

Scissors.

Sewing thread.

Pattern G   hunting waistcoat

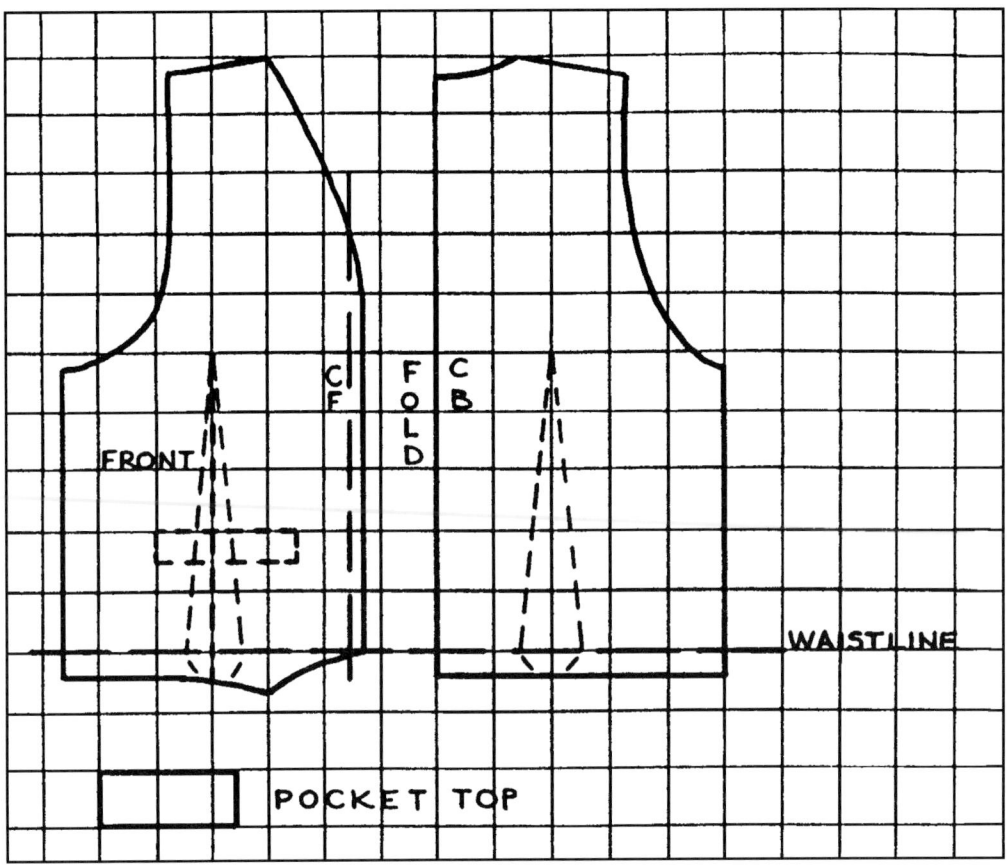

Divide length of shoulder to waist by 10 to find the height of each row.

Divide half the chest or bust measurement by 10 to find the width of each column.

Add 1.25 cm ($^1/_2$ in) all round for seam allowance.

Determine the size of darts (if any) by trying the garment on during making.

Cut around solid lines only.

To make

1. From the checked or plain material cut out one pair of front pieces.

2. From the material left at the armholes cut out two pocket tops.

3. From the lining material cut out one pair of front pieces and one pair of complete backs.

4. From the lining material left at the armholes cut out two pairs of suitably sized pocket linings.

5. Add the interfacing to the wrong side of the pocket tops and to the wrong side of the fronts in main material.

6. Place the right sides of the checked or plain material to the right side of one of the backs and join at the shoulder seam.

7. Repeat with the remaining front and back pieces in lining material.

8. Pin the side seams of the outer waistcoat and try it on inside out. Pin the front and back darts as required (if any).

9. Make identical darts in the lining.

10. Machine stitch the darts in place.

11. Fold each of the pocket tops in half along their length with the wrong sides together.

12. Place a pocket top, with a pair of pocket linings on top, at the desired position on the left outer waistcoat front. Pin and tack in place before machine stitching as shown (Fig. 26).

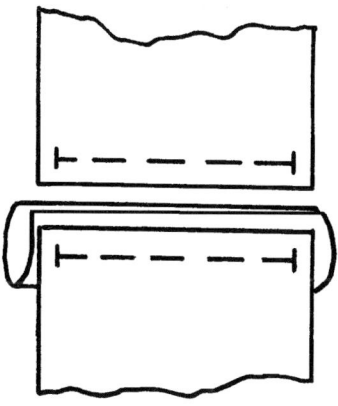

Fig. 26

13. Cut through the material to make the pocket opening as shown in Fig. 27. (The angled cuts finish at the end of the stitching.)

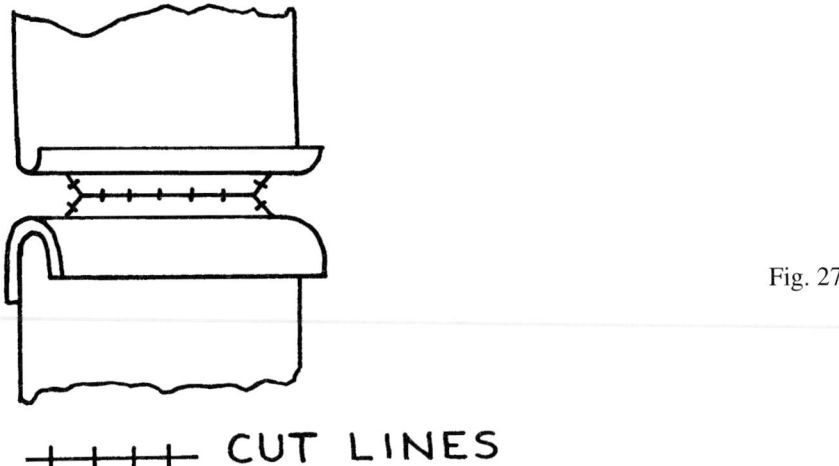

Fig. 27

┼┼┼┼ CUT LINES

14. Fold the pocket linings through to the wrong side and the pocket top into position on the right side.

15. On the wrong side, stitch around the pocket lining and across the ends of the pocket tops (Fig. 28).

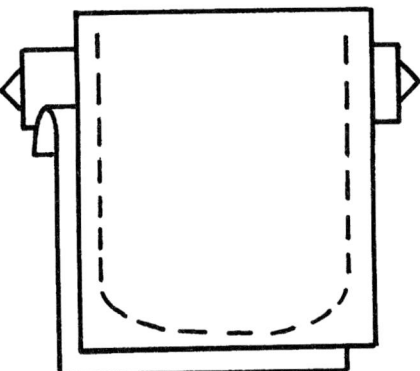

Fig. 28

16. Trim away surplus lining material from the pocket lining (Fig. 29).

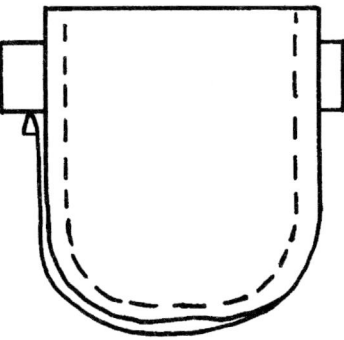

Fig. 29

17. Press the pocket top.

18. Repeat with the second pocket on the right front if required.

19. Place the right side of the outer waistcoat to the right side of the lining. Machine stitch around the armholes and around the front and neck edges (Fig. 30).

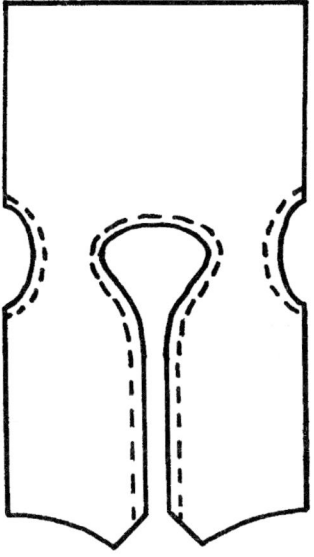

Fig. 30

20. Turn each front through the relevant shoulder so that right sides are now outermost and press.

21. Tack and then machine stitch the side seams. Press.

22. Fold under to the wrong side 1.25 cm ($^1/_2$ in) on both the outer waistcoat and the lining all the way along the lower hem. Tack and then machine stitch the two layers together 0.75 cm ($^1/_4$ in from the edge) (Fig. 31). Press.

Fig. 31

23. Add buttons and buttonholes to the appropriate sides.

Jodhpur pattern

(a pattern conversion)

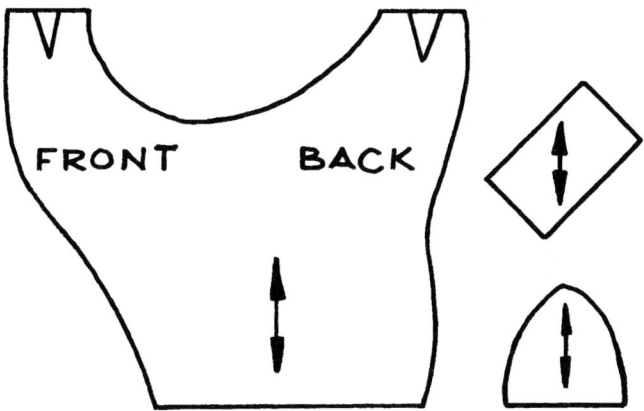

You will need

A pattern for a pair of tightly fitting trousers.

Scrap paper (such as newspaper or wallpaper) for the conversion stage.

Pattern paper or brown paper for the final pattern.

A felt-tipped pen.

Sellotape or pins.

Scissors.

To make the pattern

1. Place the pattern you are using for conversion against yourself, and ask a friend to mark on it the position of the below the knee seam of the final pattern for both the front and the back leg pieces.

2. Place the pattern on the scrap paper, and transfer all the pattern markings, except the grain arrows. **Especially mark 'front' and 'back'.**

3. Discard the original pattern.

4. Sellotape or pin together the inside leg seam on the scrap pattern, matching notches and seam lines as far as possible to keep the joined pieces flat (Fig. 32).

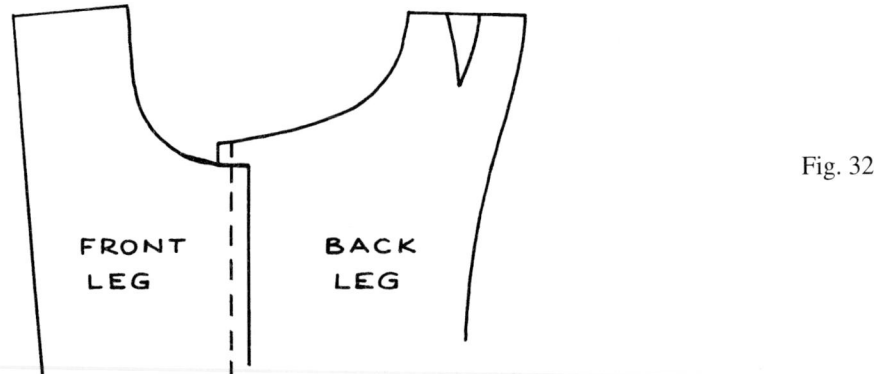

Fig. 32

5. Sellotape or pin together the outside leg seam from the lower hem up to the curve of the hip. Leave unjoined the hip shaping where this would prevent the paper from staying flat.

6. Mark and then cut the position of the new seam, starting at the unjoined hip part of the side seam, and curving to run down the front of the leg. This will cause the pattern to open out flat again (Fig. 33).

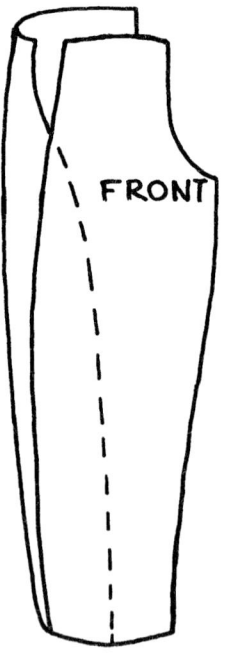

Fig. 33

7. Cut across where the knee seam is to be and mark new grain arrows as shown in Fig. 34.

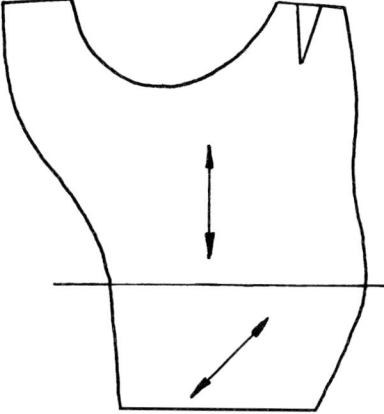

Fig. 34

8. Recut the two new pattern pieces from pattern paper or brown wrapping paper, adding the seam allowances to the new seam down the front of the leg and to the under knee seam and 7.5 cm (3 in) to the length of the calf pieces.

9. Transfer all the relevant markings to the new pattern pieces.

10. Cut out a suitably sized pattern for shaped knee patches as shown in Fig. 35 (about 27 cm [10$^1/_2$ in] by 16.5 cm [6$^1/_2$ in] for an adult).

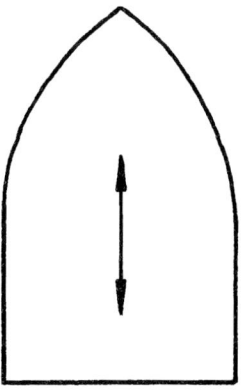

Fig. 35

11. Cut a pattern piece for the waistband 7.5 cm (3 in) wide.

Jodhpurs

(use the graph pattern or a pattern conversion)

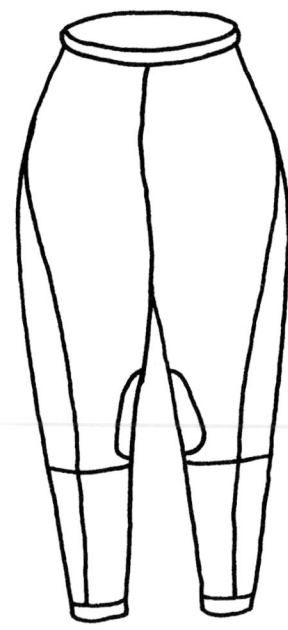

You will need

A pattern (either from the graph pattern or a pattern conversion from the previous chapter).

150 cm (50 or 60 in) wide stretch fabric the length of the finished jodhpurs plus 7.5 cm (3 in).

Waistband stiffening.

A hook and bar or a button for the waistband fastening.

A zip.

Matching sewing thread.

Pattern H jodhpurs

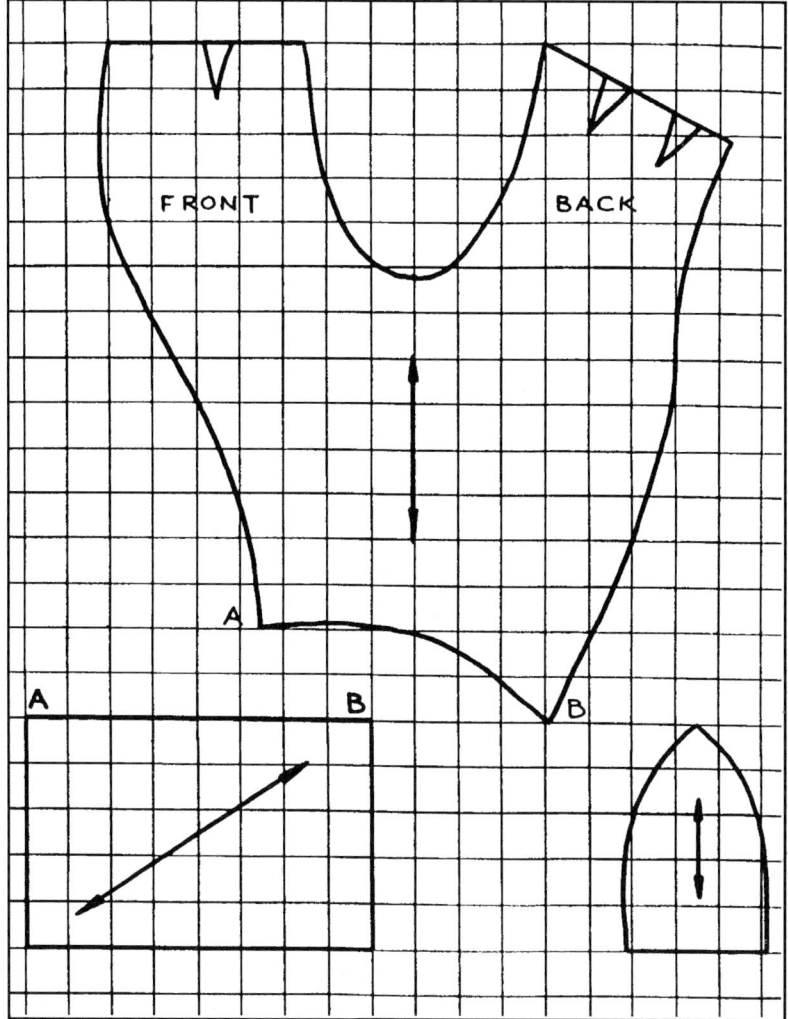

For a tight fit, add 2.5 cm (1 in) to the hip measurement.

Divide half the hip measurement by 10 to find the width of each column.

Divide the length from the waist to below the knee by 13 to find the height of each row.

Measure around the top of the calf just below the knee and make a suitably sized pleat at the centre of the line AB to make this measurement correct. Taper the pleat to a point at the crutch.

Adjust the corresponding width AB on the calf piece.

To make

1. Fold the fabric in half down its length and find a suitable layout for the pattern pieces. Cut out one pair each of the legs, calf pieces and knee patches. Cut out only one waistband.

2. Stitch and press darts.

3. Join the under the knee seams with a flat seam and then top stitch both sides of the join. (Fig. 36)

Fig. 36

4. Turn under and tack 0.75 cm ($^1/_4$ in) all the way round the knee patches. Position these just above the under the knee seam directly below the lowest point of the crutch and attach them with two rows of straight machine stitching 0.75 cm ($^1/_4$ in) apart, or with one row of straight stitching 0.75 cm ($^1/_4$ in) in from the edge and zigzag over the edge (Fig. 37).

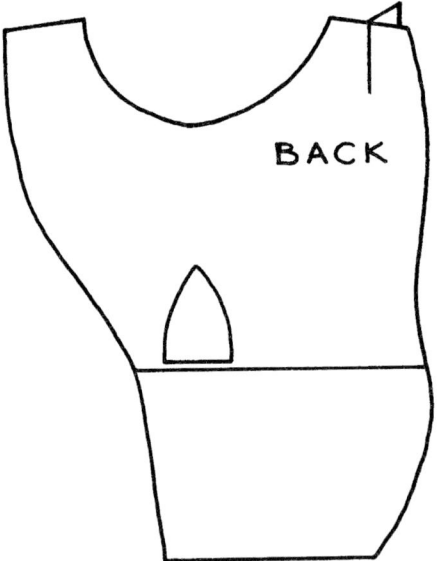

Fig. 37

5. Place right sides of the fabric together and join the side/front seam. Press it to one side away from the knee patches. Turn through to the right side, and top stitch the laid seam (Fig. 38).

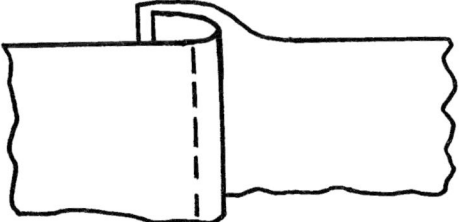

Fig. 38

6. Join the centre back/front seam. Press open and insert the zip into the front, attaching a zip-guard if you wish. (This need only be zigzagged or straight stitched close to the free raw edge.)

7. Attach the waistband and then the hook and bar or sew on a button and make a buttonhole.

8. Make a 7.5 cm (3 in) hem at the lower edge of the leg so that a cuff can be turned up when the jodhpurs are worn.

Optional extras

Strong elastic can be attached to the lower edge of the leg to pass under the instep to hold the cuffs down over the boots.

A small coin pocket can be added, being sewn in with the waistband.

Breeches pattern

(a pattern conversion)

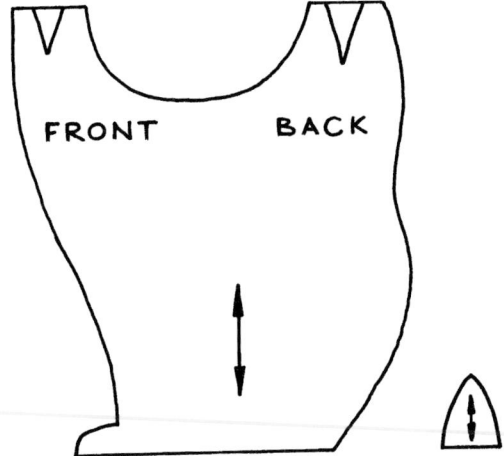

You will need

A pattern for a pair of tightly fitting trousers.

Scrap paper (such as newspaper or wallpaper) for the conversion stage.

Pattern paper or brown paper for the final pattern.

A felt-tipped pen.

Sellotape or pins.

Scissors.

To make the pattern

1. Place the pattern you are using for conversion against yourself, and ask a friend to mark on it the position of the mid-calf for both the front and the back leg pieces.

2. Place the pattern on the scrap paper, and transfer all the pattern markings, except the grain arrows. **Especially mark 'front' and 'back'.**

3. Discard the original pattern.

4. Sellotape or pin together the inside leg seam on the scrap pattern, matching notches and seam lines as far as possible to keep the joined pieces flat (Fig. 39).

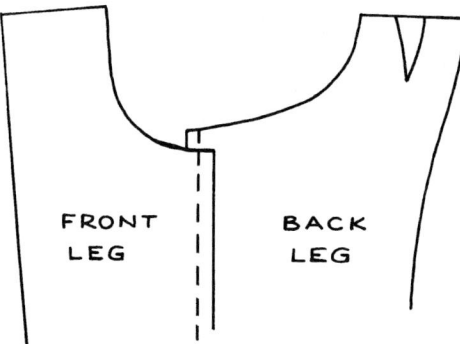

Fig. 39

5. Sellotape or pin together the outside leg seam from the lower hem up to the curve of the hip. Leave unjoined the hip shaping where this would prevent the paper from staying flat.

6. Mark and then cut the position of the new seam, starting at the unjoined hip part of the side seam, and curving to run down the front of the leg. This will cause the pattern to open out flat again (Fig. 40).

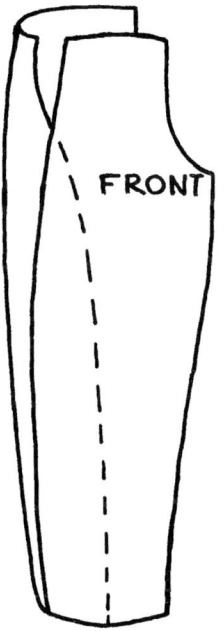

Fig. 40

7. Cut across where the mid-calf hem will be and add a 3 cm (1¼ in) tab to the front lower edge and mark a new grain arrow as shown in Fig. 41.

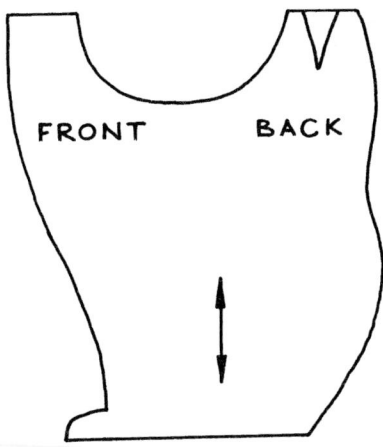

Fig. 41

8. Recut a new pattern piece from pattern paper or brown wrapping paper, adding the seam allowances to the new seam down the front of the leg.

9. Transfer all the relevant markings to the new pattern piece.

10. Cut out a suitably sized pattern for shaped knee patches as shown in Fig. 42 (about 27 cm [10½ in] by 16.5 cm [6½ in] for an adult).

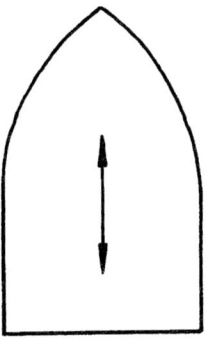

Fig. 42

11. Cut a pattern piece for the waistband 7.5 cm (3 in) wide.

Breeches

(use the graph pattern or a pattern conversion)

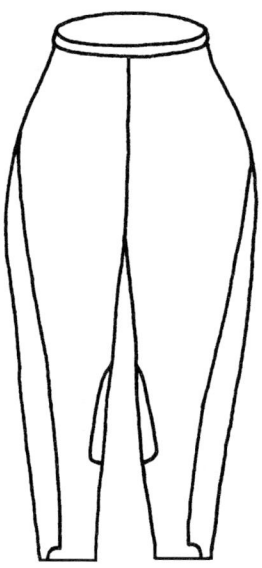

You will need

A pattern (either from the graph pattern or a pattern conversion from the previous chapter).

150 cm (50 or 60 in) wide stretch fabric the length of the finished breeches.

Waistband stiffening.

A hook and bar or a button for the waistband fastening.

A zip.

Approximately 1 m (1 yd) toning bias binding for binding the lower leg edge.

6 cm ($2^{1}/_{2}$ in) of 2.5 cm (1 in) wide Velcro.

Matching sewing thread.

Pattern I breeches

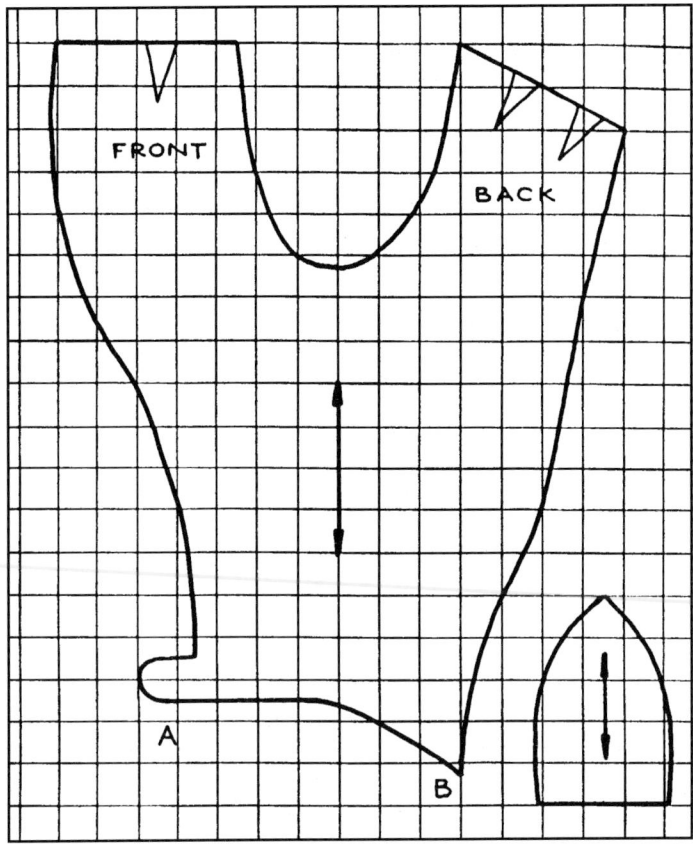

For a tight fit add 2.5 cm (1 in) to the hip measurement.

Divide half the hip measurement by 10 to find the width of each column.

Divide the length from the waist to below the knee by 15 to find the height of each row.

Measure around the mid calf and make a suitably sized pleat to reduce the width of the pattern at the middle of the line AB to make this measurement correct. Taper the pleat to a point at the crutch.

To make the breeches

1. Fold the fabric in half down its length and place the pattern pieces on it. Cut out one pair each of the legs and the knee patches. Cut out only one waistband.

2. Stitch and press darts.

3. Bind around the lower leg edge including the tab and extending 5 cm (2 in) above it and to the same level on the side without the tab (Fig. 43).

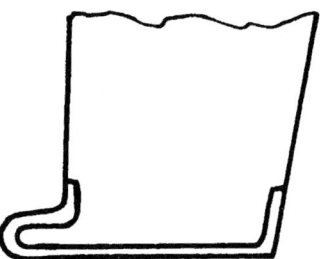

Fig. 43

4. Turn under and tack 0.75 cm (¼ in) all the way round the knee patches. Place these at the appropriate position directly below the lowest part of the crutch and attach them with two rows of straight machine stitching 0.75 cm (¼ in) apart, or with one row of straight stitching 0.75 cm (¼ in) in from the edge and zigzag over the edge (Fig. 44).

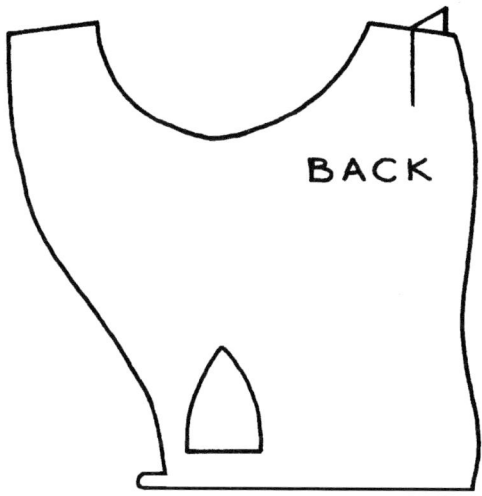

Fig. 44

5. Place right sides of the fabric together and join the side/front seam, leaving approximately 5 cm (2 in) unjoined above the tab at the lower leg edge. Press the seam to one side away from the knee patches. Turn through to the right side, and top stitch the laid seam (Fig. 45).

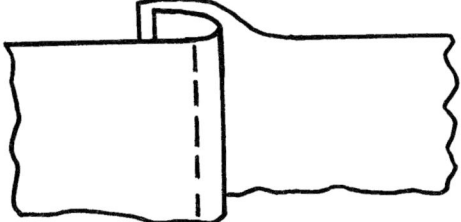

Fig. 45

6. Cut the Velcro in half and stitch one piece of hook to the tab and one piece of loop in the corresponding position on the other side of the leg opening.

7. Join the centre back/front seam. Press open and insert the zip into the front, attaching a zip-guard if you wish. (This need only be zigzagged or straight stitched close to the free raw edge.)

8. Attach the waistband and then the hook and bar or sew on a button and make a buttonhole.

Optional extra

A small coin pocket can be added, being sewn in with the waistband.

Showing/hacking jacket pattern

(a pattern adaptation)

Because of the variety and fashions in styles of lapels, collars, shaping seams and vents, it would not be sensible to include an actual pattern for a jacket. A pattern for a normal everyday jacket is unsuitable because it will not allow room for movement across the shoulders when riding. It will also be too short and the buttons and buttonholes will not be in the correct places. There are different styles for ladies and gentlemen.

A commercial pattern can, however, be easily adapted.

Choose a pattern which has the general shape and the basic styles of collar and lapels that you want. If possible, the pattern should also have the desired seam shaping and venting (one central back vent or two side vents) but these are not so important as they can be added to the pattern.

For children choose a boy's jacket as both boys and girls have similar shapes.

Shaping can be achieved either in seams or in darts – for ladies, seam shaping looks smarter.

The following are some possible styles.

Some front views

Some back views

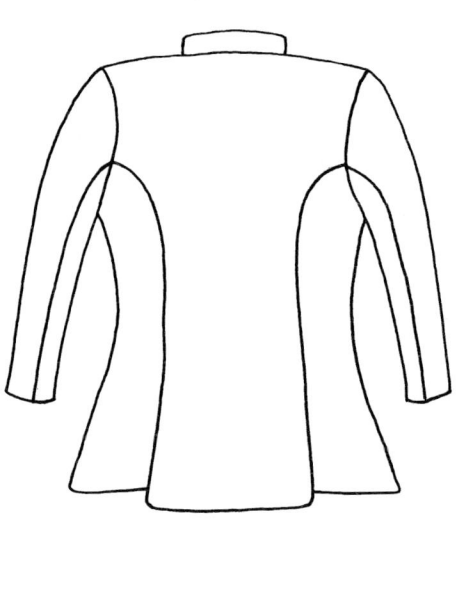

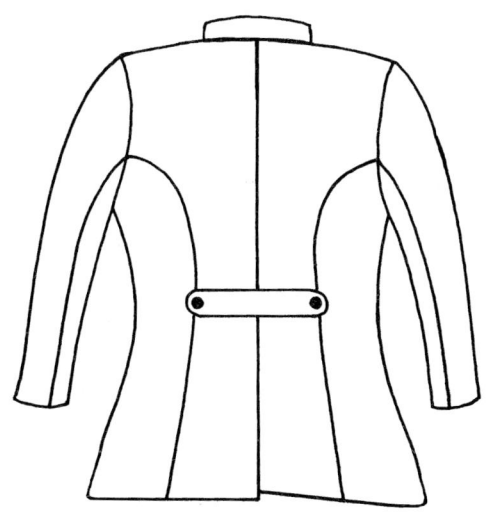

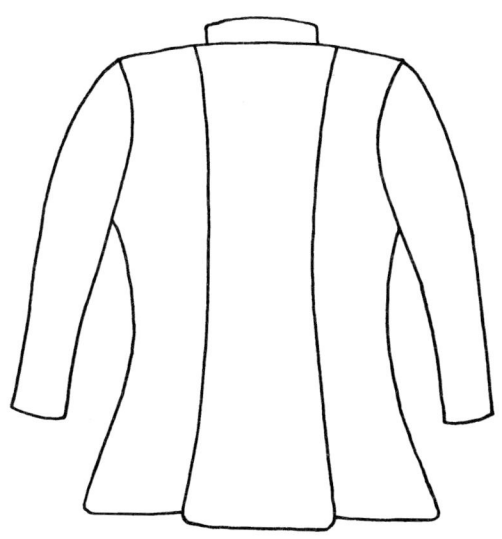

To make your pattern wide enough across the back

1. Add 0.75 cm ($^1/_4$ in) to the back armhole as shown in Fig. 46.

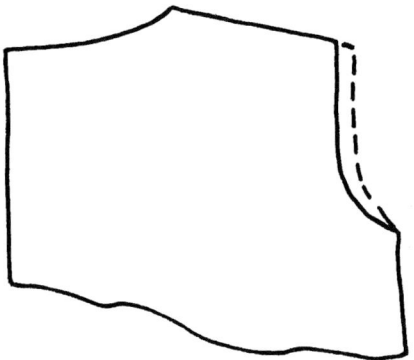

Fig. 46

To make the jacket the correct length

2. Sit on a chair and measure from the waist to the seat of the chair (Fig. 47).

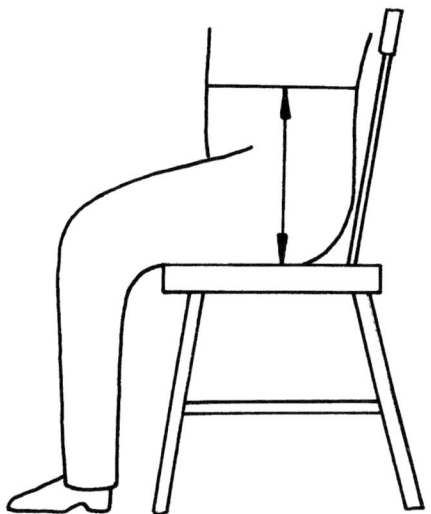

Fig. 47

3. Add the required amount to the length of the jacket – don't forget to allow for the hem.

To reposition the buttons and buttonholes

4. The lowest buttonhole should be at, or *just* above, the waist. The top buttonhole might need to be raised so that it is at half the height of the armhole. If necessary, recut the lapels to keep the front opening straight (Fig. 48).

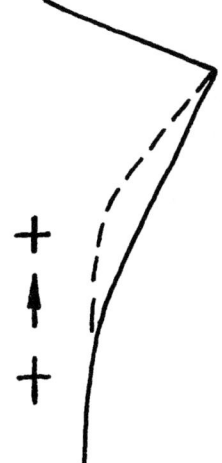

Fig. 48

To replace darts with shaping seams

5. Pin any side bust darts along the stitching line but ensure that the point of the dart ends at the point of the bust. Draw on the pattern where you want the shaping seam to be and then cut along the drawn line. (Fig. 49). When cutting out the material add 1.25 cm ($^1/_2$ in) seam allowance to each of the pattern's cut edges. Seams can be straight from the shoulder or curved from the armhole.

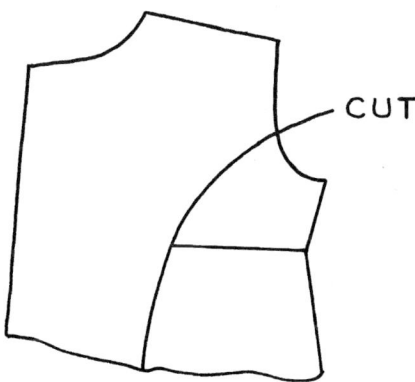

Fig. 49

To add vents

6. For a central vent, add an allowance to the centre back seam. For two side vents, add the allowance to the side back seams (Fig. 50). Vents extend up to the waist. A seam allowance for the vents has already been included. Although it will not all be needed, add the same allowance for vents to the lining – the excess can be trimmed away during making up.

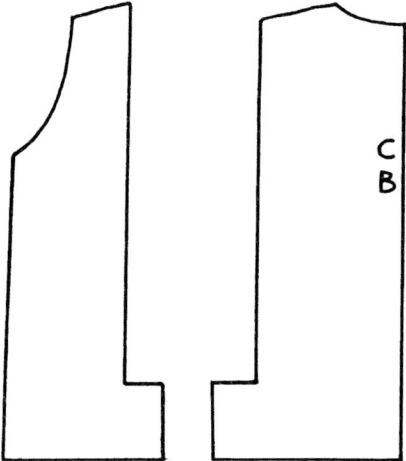

Fig. 50

To make a two-piece sleeve from a one-piece

7. Draw a line down each side of the sleeve 5 cm (2 in) from the seam line at the top and 2.5 cm (1 in) at the bottom (Fig. 51) unless there are shaping seams in the body (see step 11 – Fig. 54). Cut the two sides off the sleeve.

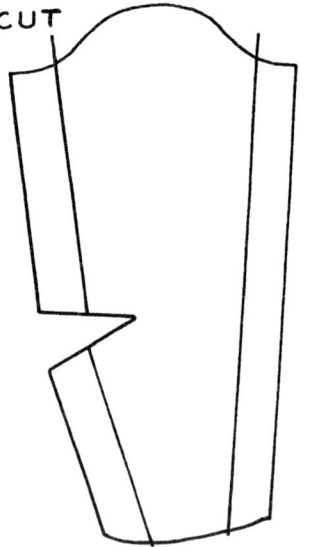

Fig. 51

8. Join the gap where the dart was on one piece. Place the two seam lines together and join the two pieces (Fig. 52).

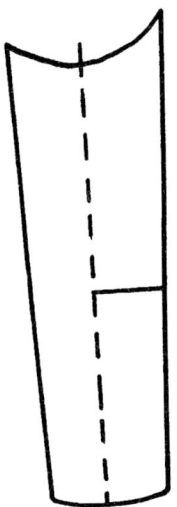

Fig. 52

9. Add a seam allowance of 1.25 cm ($^{1}/_{2}$ in) to both sides of the main sleeve piece and to both sides of the cut piece.

10. Add an allowance to the opening for button cuffs to the back seam of the new piece if required (Fig. 53). There is no need to add an allowance to the other edge since the opening will be held closed by the buttons. Make the opening in the same way as a vent.

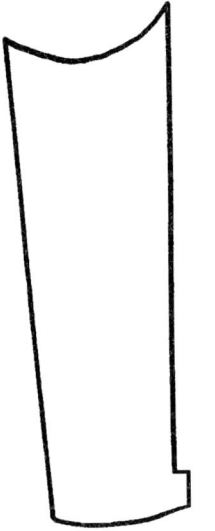

Fig. 53

11. If there are shaping seams running into the armhole, make the cut lines in the sleeve so that they meet the shaping seam in the body (Fig. 54).

Fig. 54

To allow for shoulder pads

12. If the jacket pattern does not include shoulder pads, add 0.75 cm ($^1/_4$ in) to the height of the sleeve edge of both front and back body pieces and 1.25 cm ($^1/_2$ in) to the height of the top of the sleeve (Fig. 55).

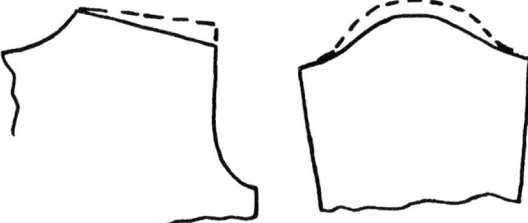

Fig. 55

Showing/hacking jacket – to make

(from an adapted pattern)

You will need

An adapted pattern.

The amount of fabric and lining material stated in the pattern plus the amount added to the jacket length.

A small piece of matching velvet for the top of the collar if desired.

Sufficient buttons for front, cuff openings and back belt (if added).

Shoulder pads.

Interfacing for front edge, pockets, collar and cuffs.

To make

It is essential to keep a hot iron and damp cloth to hand so that you can press each seam as you work.

Follow the instructions included with the pattern, but make the following additions/alterations as you get to the appropriate place in the making up.

To top-stitch shaping seams

1. On the underside flatten the seam towards the centre of the body or away from the back on the sleeves. For a centre back seam running into a vent flatten the seam so that the vent is pointing in the right direction: left side on top (Fig. 56).

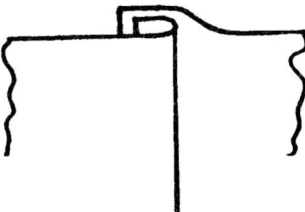

Fig. 56

2. Press and then top stitch (Fig. 57).

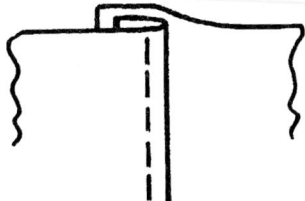

Fig. 57

To add vents

3. Stitch the seam from the shoulder or armhole edge, depending on the style chosen, down to the top of the vent opening. Snip into the end of the seam and press both parts of the vent to the appropriate side: towards the centre back seam for side vents, towards the left side seam for a central vent. Press the seam open for a flat seam or in the same direction as the vent if the seam is to be top-stitched (Fig. 58).

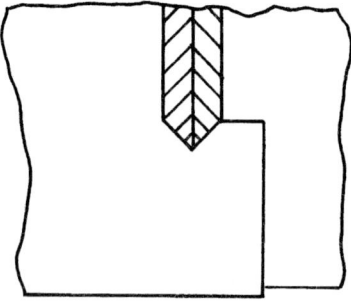

Fig. 58

4. Fold to the wrong side the appropriate amount of seam allowance and press (Fig. 59).

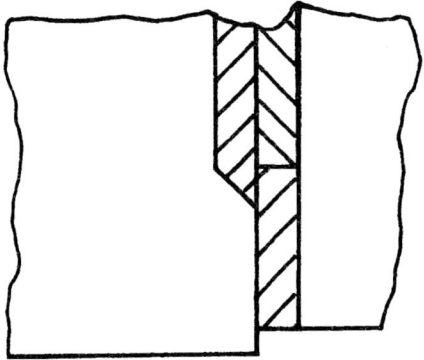

Fig. 59

5. When the lining is being added to the jacket, trim away excess lining material from top layer of vent, pin and then hand stitch the lining to the vent opening (Fig. 60).

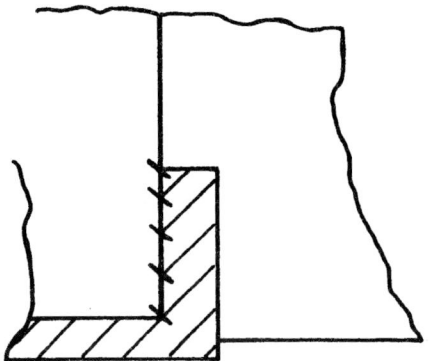

Fig. 60

To add cuff openings

6. Stitch the seam from the shoulder edge down to the top of the cuff opening. Snip into the end of the seam and press both parts of the opening towards the centre of the sleeve. Press the seam open for a flat seam or in the same direction as the opening if the seam is to be top-stitched (Fig. 61).

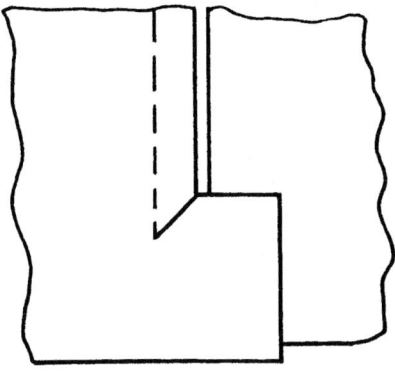

Fig. 61

7. Fold to the wrong side the appropriate amount of seam allowance and press (Fig. 62).

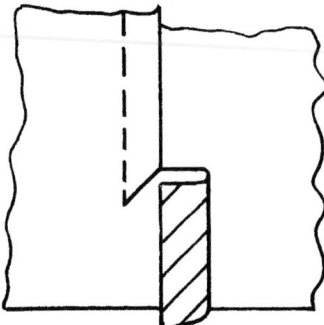

Fig. 62

8. Before the lining is added to the jacket, add a strip of iron-on interfacing inside the cuff hem and press (Fig. 63). Trim away excess lining material from top layer of the opening. Pin and then hand stitch the lining to the cuff opening.

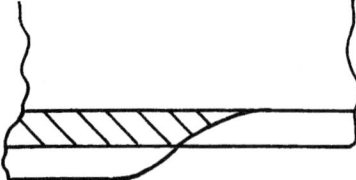

Fig. 63

9. Add buttons through all layers of the cuff opening.

To add a velvet collar

10. Cut the top collar from velvet, ensuring that the nap (pile) lays down the centre back of the collar (Fig. 64).

Fig. 64

To add shoulder pads

11. Once the sleeves have been inserted in the armholes, insert the shoulder pads with the centre line of the pad running along the shoulder seam. Hand stitch the pad in place at the three points indicated in Fig. 65.

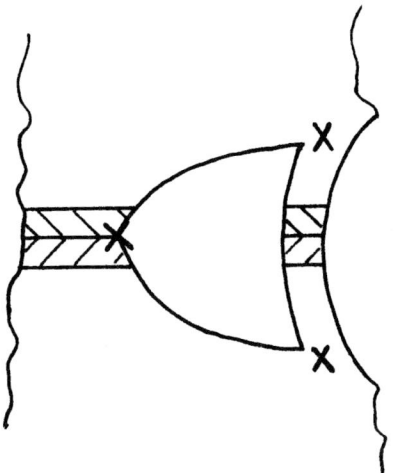

Fig. 65

To add a false belt to the centre back as shown at the top of page 47

12. Before the lining is added to the jacket, cut out a piece of fabric the length and width required, but add 1.25 cm ($^1/_2$ in) all round for seam allowance.

13. Cut out a piece of interfacing without seam allowance.

14. Place the interfacing on the wrong side of the fabric, turn in the seam allowance all around, tack in place, and press (Fig. 66).

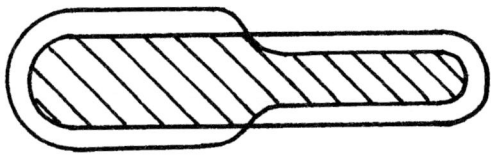

Fig. 66

15. Remove the tacking stitches. Place the false belt in its final position on the jacket and tack before stitching all round 0.75 cm ($^1/_4$ in) from the edge.

16. After the jacket is finished, add buttons and buttonholes.

Crash hat cover with six segments

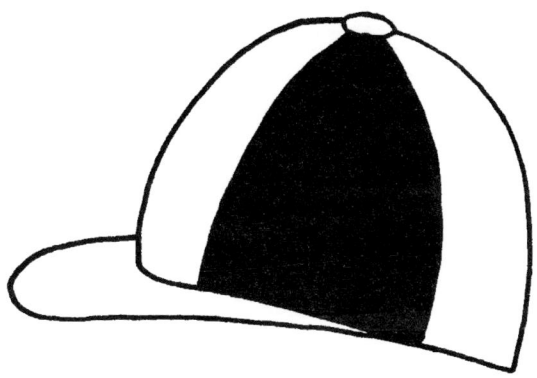

You will need

0.5 m (½ yd) satin or velvet for the top layer.

0.5 m (½ yd) white cotton for the lining.

Piece of flat, flexible plastic (e.g. the side of a plastic drinks container) 18 cm (7½ in) by 12 cm (4¾ in).

A button to cover.

0.5 m (½ yd) of 0.75 cm (¼ in) wide elastic.

Sewing thread to match all the colours of the top layer.

To make

1. Measure around the circumference at the lower edge of the crash hat, then from the centre back edge to the centre top and from the centre front edge to the centre top (Fig. 67).

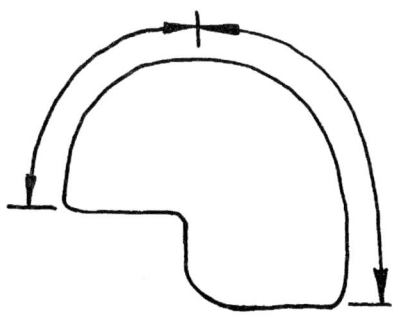

Fig. 67

Pattern J   crash hat cover with six segments

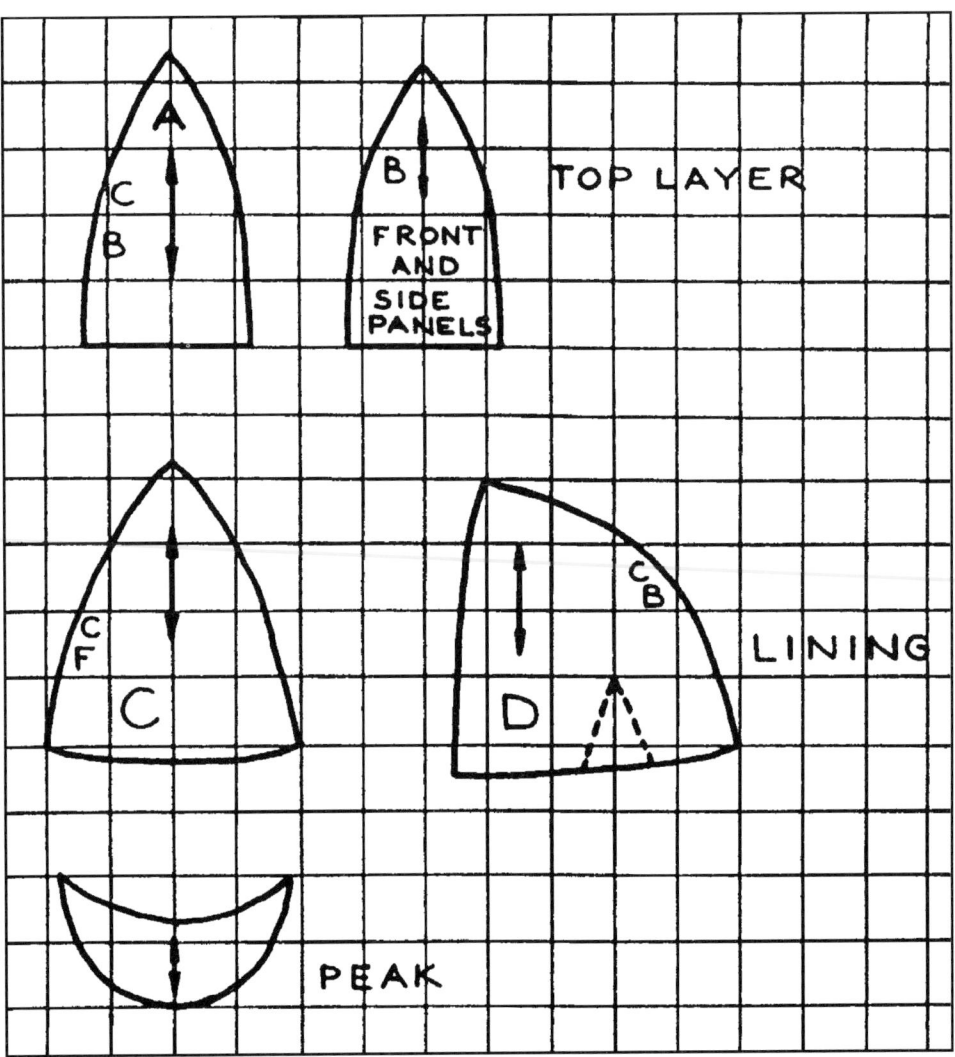

Divide the circumference of the hat by 16 to find the size of each square. Check the pattern against the hat measurements.

For multicolours make sure the segment colours are cut out correctly.

For a velvet cover ensure the direction of the nap (pile) lines up with the grain arrows and runs from the top of the cover to the edge.

Add 1.25 cm ($^1/_2$ in) seam allowance all around. Cut four of piece B and two of all other pieces.

2. Join one of piece A and two of piece B for the top layer using a fraction less of the seam allowance to allow the cover to fit over the hat, making sure that the colours are in the correct order and then press the seams towards the outer edge. Top-stitch the seams (Fig. 68).

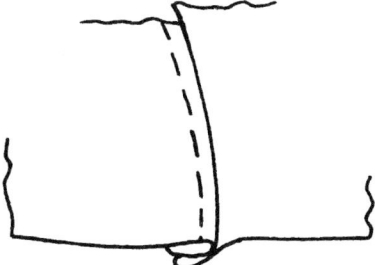

Fig. 68

3. Repeat with the remaining pieces, making sure that this side is a mirror image of the other, and that if different colours are used, they are in the correct order.

4. Join the two halves together, press the seam to one side and top-stitch.

5. Cover the button and stitch at the centre.

6. For the lining, join one piece C to one piece D and then repeat with the other pair, again making sure that a mirror image is produced. Press the seams open.

7. Join the two sides of the lining together, leaving a gap of approximately 10 cm (4 in) open towards one end (Fig. 69).

Fig. 69

8. Stitch around the outer edge of the pair of peak pieces, right sides together (Fig. 70).

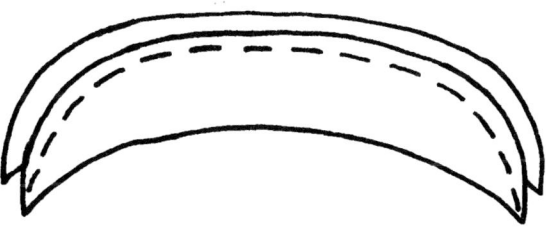

Fig. 70

9. Turn the peak through to the right side and top-stitch the seam to the underside of the peak.

10. Insert the plastic into the peak.

11. Place the peak on the edge of the top layer at the front, with the peak pointing to the button and with the top-stitching uppermost. Pin in place close to the edge of the plastic (Fig. 71).

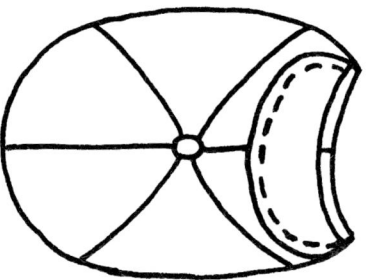

Fig. 71

12. Cut a strip of the same material used for the peak 6.5 cm ($2^1/_2$ in) wide, long enough to go around the remainder of the edge of the cover plus 5 cm (2 in) to overlap the peak. Fold it in half with the right side outermost.

13. Stitch along its length 1.25 cm ($^1/_2$ in) from the raw edges. Insert the elastic, pull it slightly to form a slight gather and stitch across the ends of the elastic to secure it.

14. Pin the strip around the edge of the top layer, pulling it straight, with the folded edge pointing towards the button. Overlap the peak with the ends of the strip (Fig. 72).

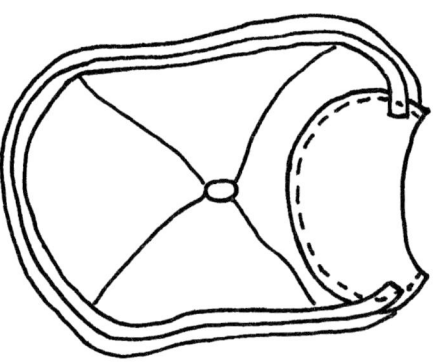

Fig. 72

15. Matching centre back and centre front, place the right side of the lining on to the right side of the top layer (over the top of the edging strip and peak), making a pleat in each of the back segments at the places marked on the pattern. Machine stitch all around the edge so that the peak and the edging strip are included in the seam, trapped between the two layers of the cover.

16. Turn the cover through to the right side through the opening left in the lining.

17. Fold in the raw edges of the opening and machine stitch it closed (Fig. 73).

Fig. 73

Crash hat cover – other designs

Four segments

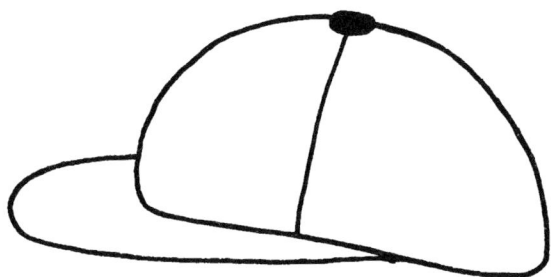

1. Cut both top layer and lining using the lining pattern (see pattern J on page 60).

2. In the top-layer material, join one piece C and one piece D, press the seams towards the back and top-stitch.

3. Repeat with the other pair.

4. Follow steps 4 to 14 for the six-segment cover.

5. Matching centre back and centre front, place the right side of the lining on to the right side of the top layer (over the top of the edging strip and peak), making a pleat in each of the lining back segments at the places marked on the pattern, but easing the edge of the top layer to fit. Machine stitch all around the edge so that the peak and the edging strip are included in the seam, trapped between the two layers of the cover.

6. Follow steps 16 and 17 for the six-segment cover.

Stripes

1. Using a piece of scrap cotton, make up the top layer only (without the button) of the six-segment cover in the previous chapter and press the seams flat.

2. Place the cover over the hat. Using a felt-tipped pen, draw on the stripes, and number each stripe to make sure they are put together in the correct order. Cut the cover into strips along the drawn lines. Use this as a pattern for the striped top layer, cutting the strips with the grain running across the centre of each strip, and remembering to add 1.25 cm ($^1/_2$ in) seam allowance to both sides of each.

3. Join the seams, press them towards the edge of the hat and top-stitch.

4. Make up the remainder of the cover, following steps 5 to 17 of the six-segment cover.

With a star

1. Follow steps 1 to 4 of the six-segment cover.

2. Cut a star pattern and then cut out from the required colour of top layer material with the grain running down the centre line of the hat. Add 1.25 cm ($^1/_2$ in) seam allowance.

3. Place the cover over the hat and ease the star into place so that it fits correctly. Pin and then tack in position.

4. Remove the cover from the hat and machine top-stitch the star in place.

5. Follow steps 5 to 17 of the six-segment cover.

Checked

1. This is very tricky, but it can be done. Using a piece of scrap cotton, make up the top layer only (without the button) of the six-segment cover in the previous chapter and press the seams flat.

2. Place it on the crash hat and, with a felt-tipped pen, draw the checked design on it and number each square.

3. Cut out the squares. Use them as a pattern for the checked top layer, remembering to add 1.25 cm ($^1/_2$ in) seam allowance all round each piece, and keeping the grain of the fabric running in the same direction across each square. Keep each numbered pattern piece pinned to the top layer material until it has been assembled to make sure they go together in the correct order.

4. Join each seam and top-stitch it as you work.

5. Make up the remainder of the cover, following steps 5 to 17 of the six-segment cover.

Other designs can be achieved by making up the six-segment cover in white cotton to get the best fit, drawing the design required in felt-tipped pen and then cutting out new pattern pieces.

Racing silk

Racing colours are registered with Weatherbys Group Ltd. and are exclusive to the owner.

First take the following measurements:

a) chest or bust measurement;
b) the distance from the back neck edge to the bottom edge of finished garment;
c) the length of your arm from shoulder to wrist taken while your forearm is folded across your waist.

Add 5 cm (2 in) to the bust or chest measurement for ease of fit plus a further 5 cm (2 in) for movement before cutting the pattern. Add the same amount to the distance round the upper arm.

You will need

Sufficient suitable fabric to make the silk in the colours of your choice.

If stripes or checks are to be used, make up striped or checked pieces of fabric before cutting out from the pattern pieces.

If bands of colour are to be included, cut across or down the pattern pieces at the appropriate points and add seam allowances to the cuts.

If shapes are to be employed (e.g. circles, star, cross) allow sufficient fabric to cut these out in addition to the main pieces and stitch them on top of the main pattern piece before you make the garment up.

Interfacing for collar and cuffs.

Buttons.

Sewing thread.

Pattern K   racing silk body

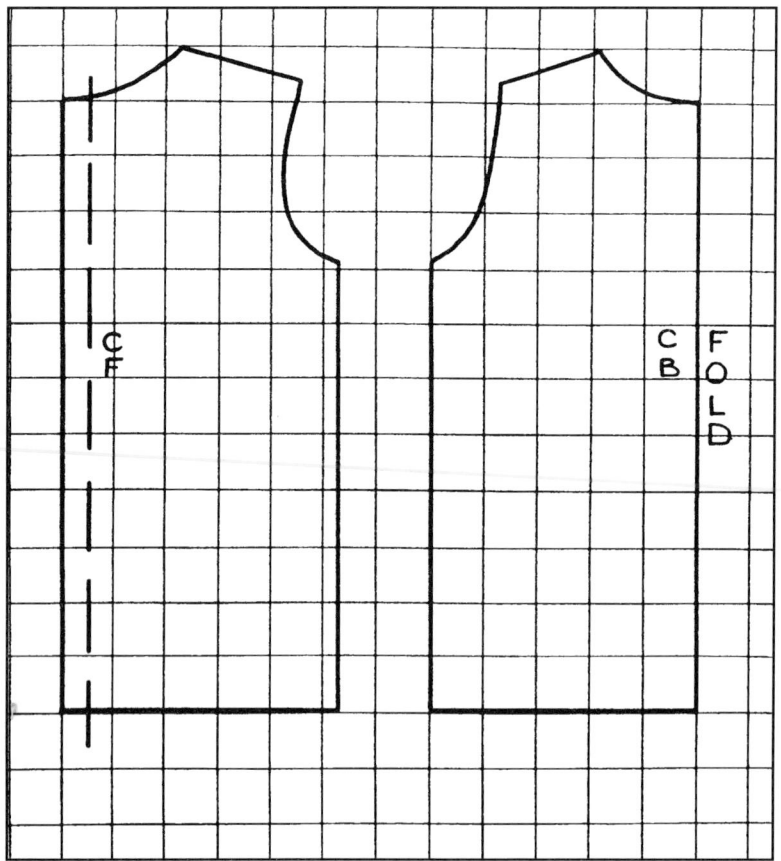

Divide finished length by 12 to find the height of each row.

Divide half the finished chest or bust measurement by 10 to find the width of each column.

Add 1.25 cm ($^1/_2$ in) all around finished pattern for seam allowance and 3.75 cm ($1^1/_2$ in) for hem at centre front and lower edge.

Pattern L   racing silk sleeve, collar and cuffs

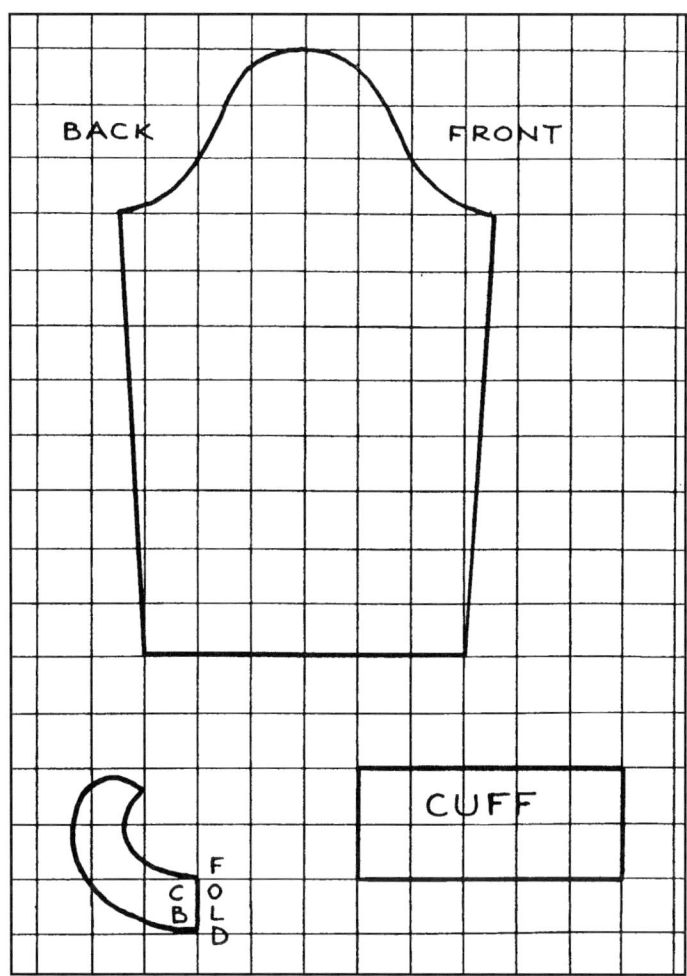

Divide finished length by 11 to find the height of each row.

Divide the finished distance round the upper arm by 7 to find the width of each column.

Add 1.25 cm ($^1/_2$ in) all around finished pattern for seam allowance.

To make

1. Cut out pieces to make up one back piece, a pair of front pieces, one pair of collar pieces and two cuffs in the main fabric. Cut out one collar piece and one cuff in interfacing. Cut the interfacing for the cuff in half down its length to provide interfacing for two cuffs. Cut out any shapes in the design, adding 1.25 cm ($^1/_2$ in) seam allowance all around the shape, plus extra for the centre front closing if appropriate as shown in Fig. 74.

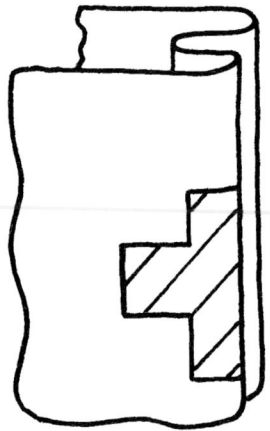

Fig. 74

2. Join together any pieces which have been cut to make up main pattern pieces (Fig. 75).

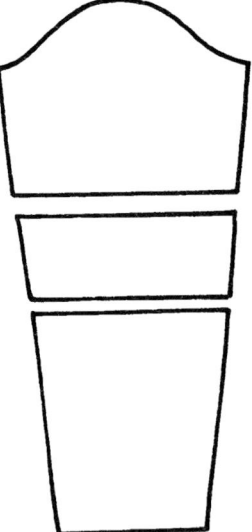

Fig. 75

3. Press seams towards the bottom of the garment if horizontal, or towards side seams if vertical. Neaten the seams and top-stitch (Fig. 76).

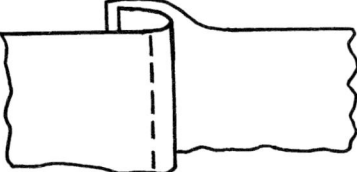

Fig. 76

4. Turn the seam allowance on any shapes under to the wrong side, press and tack in place on the appropriate main pattern fabric piece(s). Top-stitch the shapes in place.

5. Join the shoulder seams, press open and neaten.

6. Place the right sides of the two collar pieces together. Place the collar interfacing on top and stitch together around the outside. Trim away part of the seam allowances (Fig. 77).

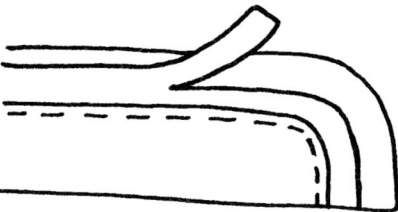

Fig. 77

7. Turn the collar through to the right side and press.

8. Fold in the hem at the centre front edges of the body and stitch down their lengths.

9. Fold in the raw edges of the collar at the neck edge and press.

10. Place the collar over the raw edge at the neck so that the edge of the collar is level with the front edge of the body, tack and then top stitch in place. Also top-stitch around the remaining edges of the collar (Fig. 78).

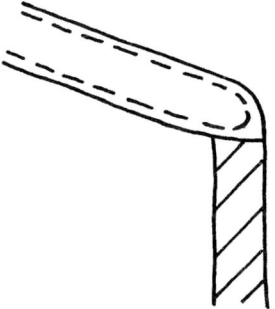

Fig. 78

11. At both lower edges of the sleeve side seams, turn in to the wrong side the seam allowance and make a hem for about 7.5 cm (3 in) (Fig. 79).

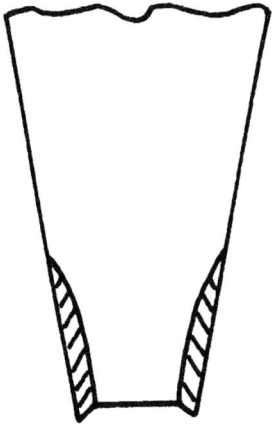

Fig. 79

12. Fold each cuff in half along its length with the right sides inside, place the interfacing on top and stitch across both ends, and snip off the corners and part of the seam allowance (Fig. 80).

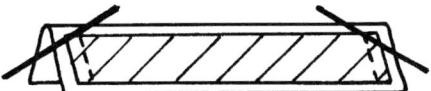

Fig. 80

13. Fold the cuffs through to the right side and press.

14. Run a gathering thread through the lower edges of the sleeves so that they fit inside the cuffs with 1.75 cm ($^3/_4$ in) of the cuff protruding at each side.

15. Fold the raw edges of the cuffs in to the wrong side and press. Place the cuffs over the gathered lower edges of the sleeves, tack and then top-stitch in place (Fig. 81).

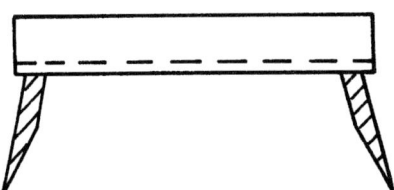

Fig. 81

16. Stitch the sleeves into the armholes.

17. Join the side seams from the lower hem of the body through the underarm down to within about 7.5 cm (3 in) of the cuff, where the sides of the sleeves were hemmed (Fig. 82).

Fig. 82

18. Hem the lower edge of the body.

19. Sew on the buttons and make buttonholes in the cuffs and down the front opening.

20. When worn, hold the edges of the collar together with a tie pin.

Chaps

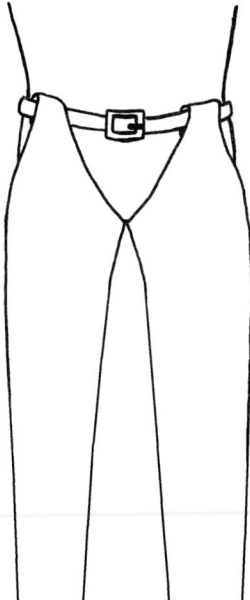

First take the following measurements:

a) wear a belt and measure the length from the bottom of the belt to the bottom edge of the chaps;

b) distance round the widest part of the thigh plus 7.5 cm (3 in);

c) length from the waist to the bottom of the buttock.

You will need

Sufficient waxed cotton, soft leather or other waterproof material to make the chaps.

The same amount of a suitable lining material.

Two open-ended zips long enough to fit the outside leg openings.

Sewing thread.

A leather-point sewing machine needle if using soft leather.

A belt.

Pattern M chaps

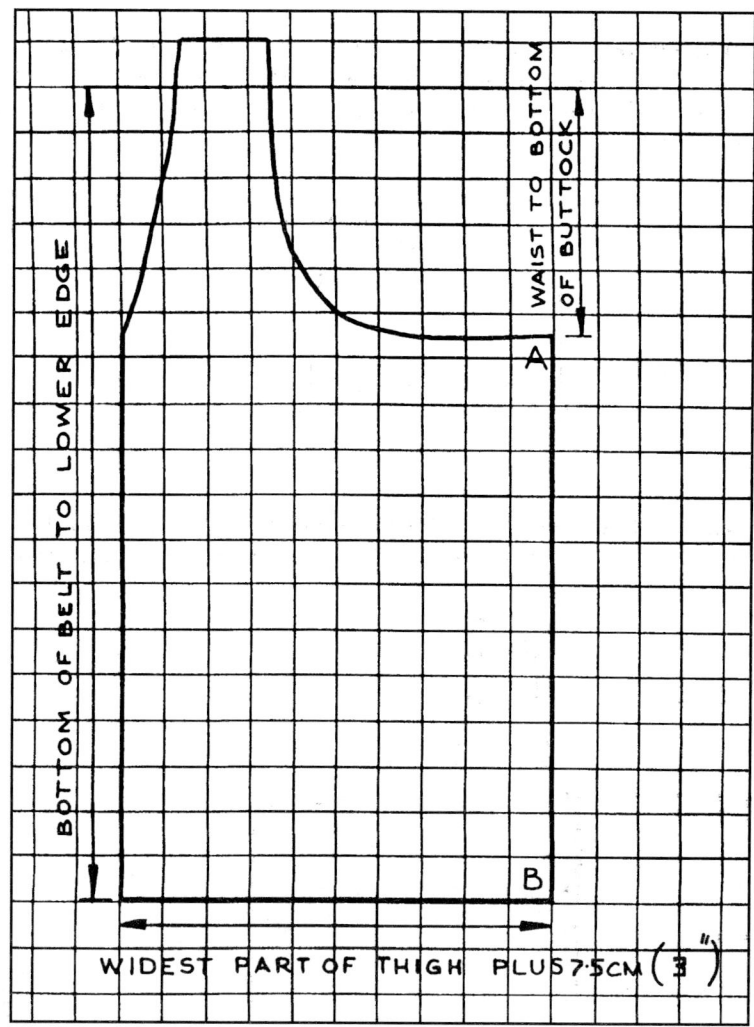

Divide the finished length by 18 to find the height of each row.

Divide the measurement around the thigh plus 7.5 cm (3 in) by 10 to find the width of each column.

Adjust the curve around the buttock to suit your own measurement.

Add 1.25 cm ($^1/_2$ in) all around for seam allowance **except** for top layer in soft leather.

To make

1. Cut out one pair in top layer material and one pair in lining material. Deal with one leg at a time.

2. **If using soft leather**, fold in the seam allowance all around the lining material and press. Place the wrong side of the lining to the wrong side of the leather so that the fold of the seam allowance of the lining is level with the cut edge of the leather. Stitch all around close to the edge (Fig. 83).

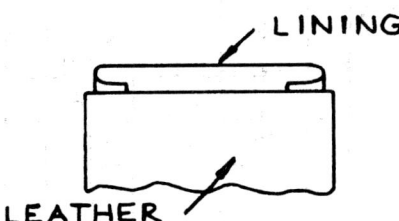

Fig. 83

3. **If using anything other than soft leather**, place the right side of the lining to the right side of the outer layer and stitch around all sides except the side marked AB on the pattern (Fig. 84).

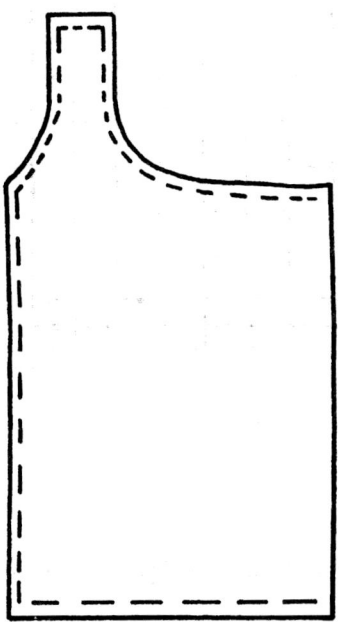

Fig. 84

4. Snip off the corners. Turn through to the right side and press all round the edges from the lining side.

5. Fold over to the wrong side 3.5 cm (1 1/2 in) at the waist to make a belt loop, and stitch (Fig. 85).

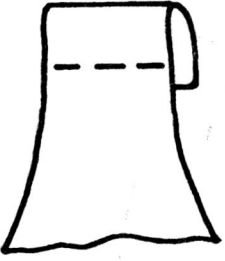

Fig. 85

6. Turn in the seam allowance along the raw edges of the open side and press.

7. Insert the zip in the side seam so that it zips from the ankle upwards (Fig. 86).

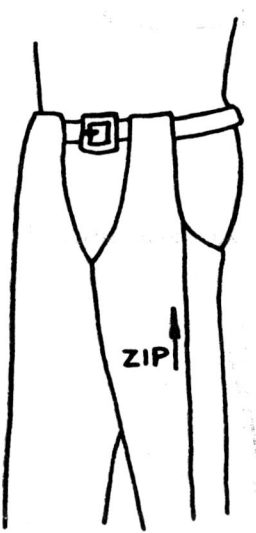

Fig. 86

8. Repeat with the other leg.

9. Thread the belt through the waist loops.

Culottes

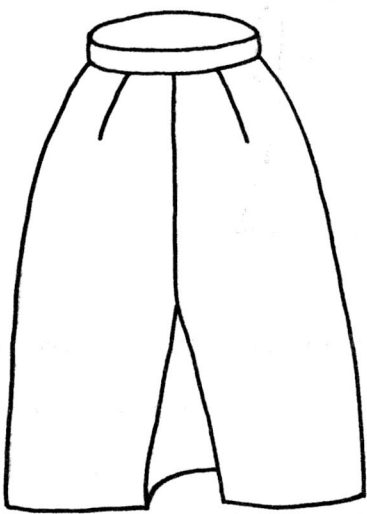

First take the following measurements:

1. Sit on a chair and take the measurement from the waist to the seat of the chair (Fig. 87);

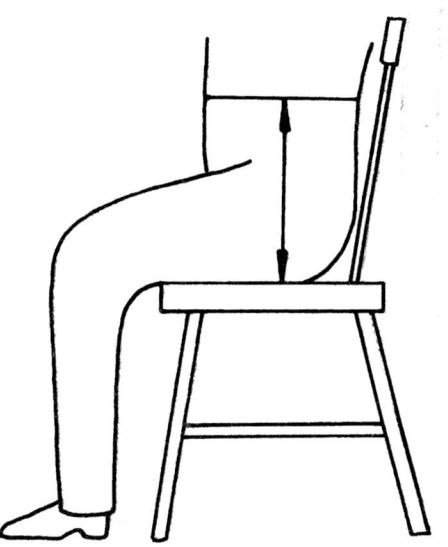

Fig. 87

2. Measure the waist, the hips at the widest part (approximately 17.5 cm (7 in) down from the waist) and from the waist to the lower hem of the finished culottes (Fig. 88).

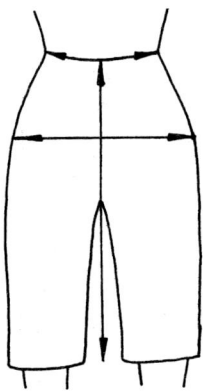

Fig. 88

You will need

150 cm (50 or 60 in) wide fabric twice the length of the finished culottes plus 5 cm (2 in).

Interfacing for the waistband.

A button or hook fastening for the waistband.

A 17.5 cm (7 in) zip.

To make

A pleat can be inserted in the back of the culottes by adding the same pleat allowance to the back pattern as for the front.

Neaten all seams and press as you work.

1. Join along the line XY on the front. Top-stitch the pleat if required by pressing the seam open and top-stitching each side of the seam.

2. Join the centre front and centre back seams (Fig. 89).

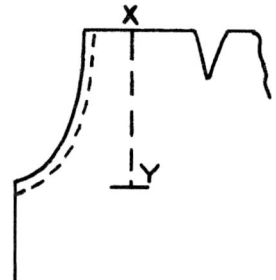

Fig. 89

Pattern N   culottes (back)

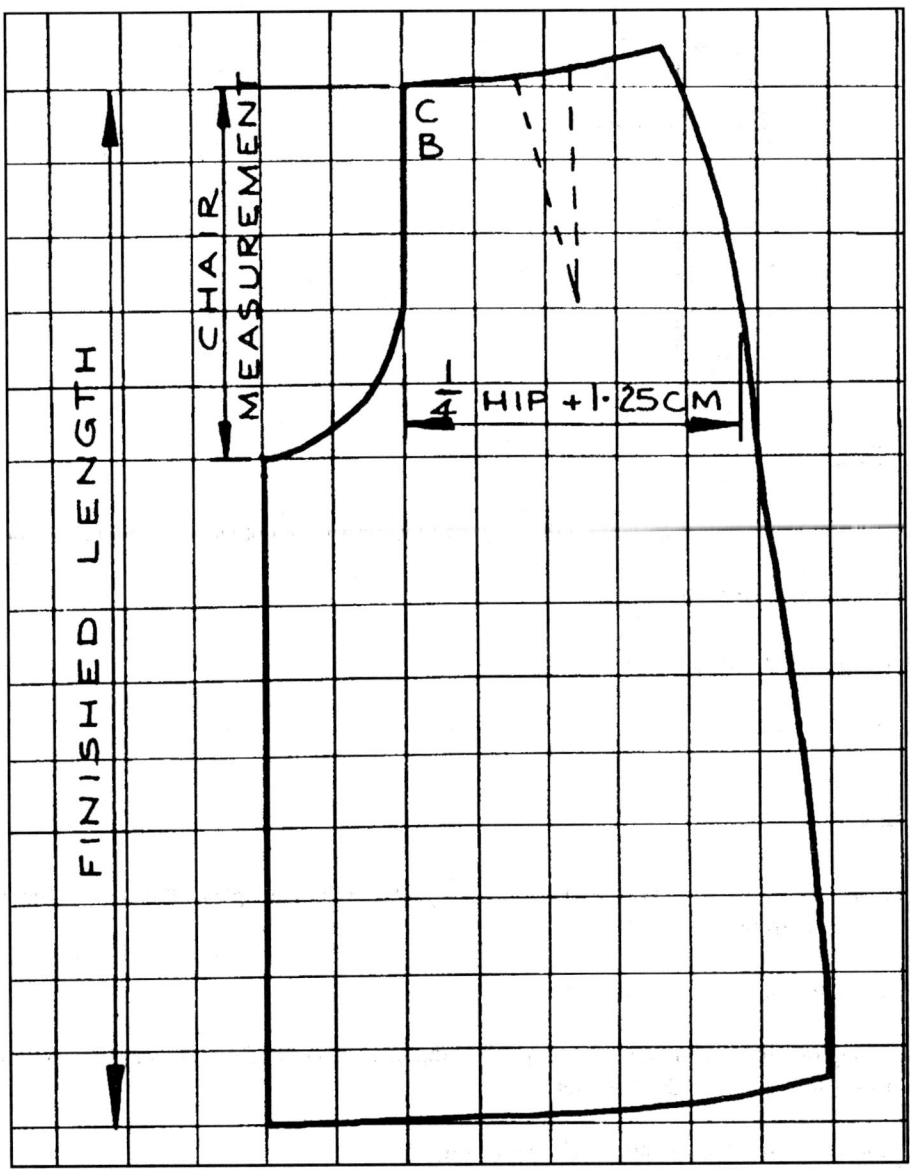

Add 1.25 cm ($^1/_2$ in) seam allowance all round.

Add 2.5 cm (1 in) hem allowance.

Pattern O culottes (front)

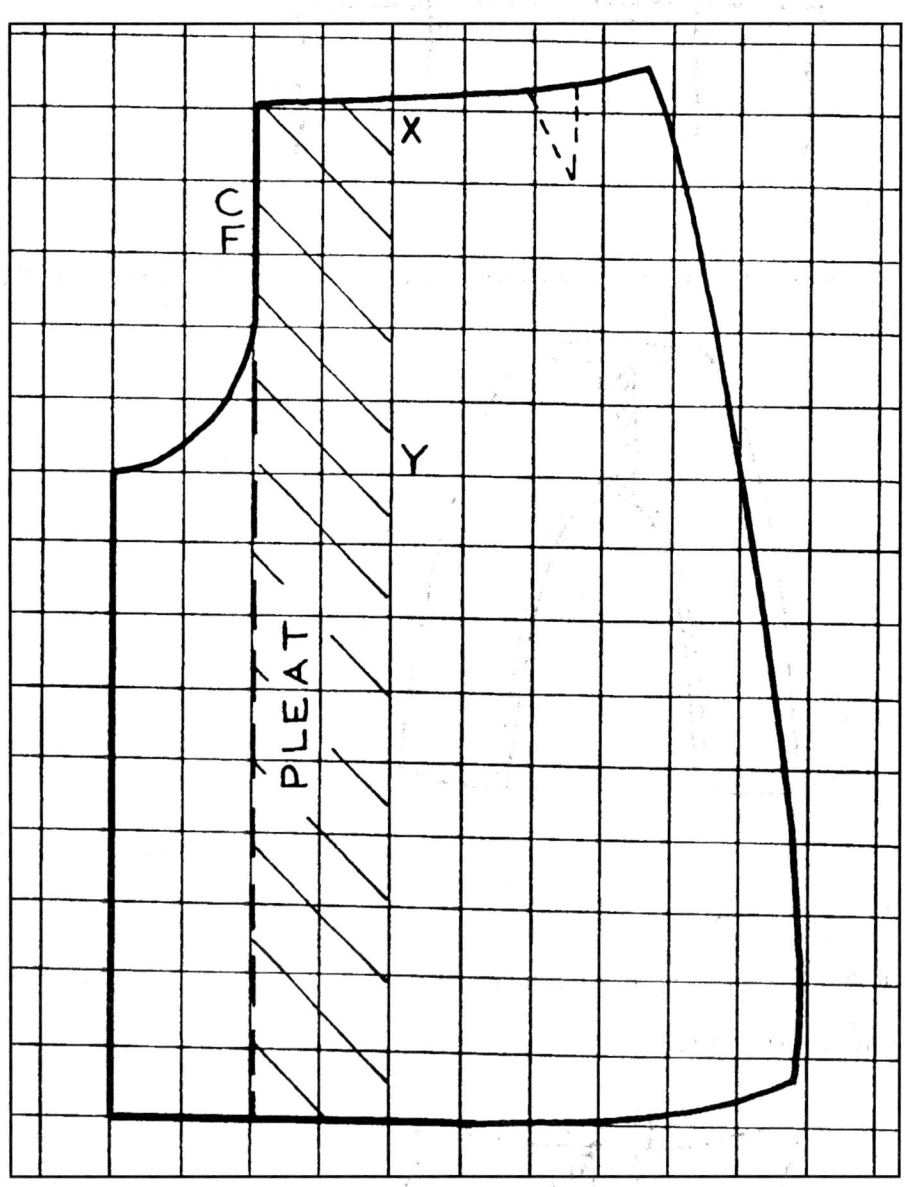

Add 1.25 cm (½ in) all round for seam allowance.

Add 2.5 cm (1 in) hem allowance.

3. Make the pleats and darts. Press and stitch in place (Fig. 90).

Fig. 90

4. Join the inside leg seam from one lower hem, through the crutch and down to the other hem (Fig. 91).

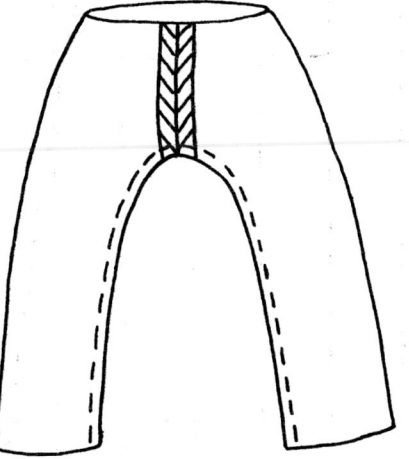

Fig. 91

5. Join the right side seam.

6. Join the left side seam up to the zip opening.

7. Insert the zip (Fig. 92).

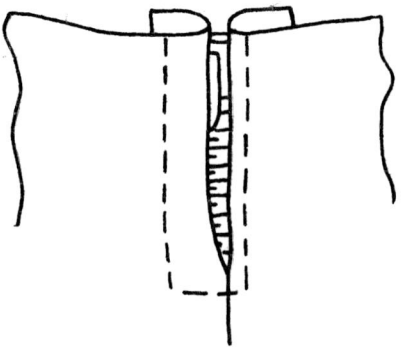

Fig. 92

8. Cut a waistband 6 cm (2½ in) longer than the waist measurement. Insert the interfacing into it. Fold the waistband in half down its length and stitch across the two short ends. Snip off the corners (Fig. 93).

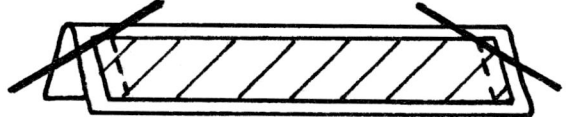

Fig. 93

9. Turn the waistband through to the right side and press.

10. Place the waistband over the top of the culottes. Pin, tack and then stitch the waistband in place with 3.5 cm (1½ in) extending beyond the zip on the front side seam (Fig. 94).

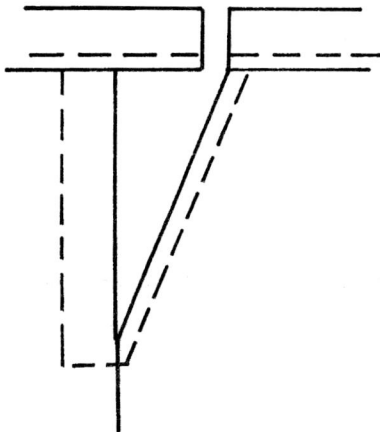

Fig. 94

11. Add a button and buttonhole or hook and bar.

12. Hem the lower edges of the legs.

Soft leather hat

First take or decide the following measurements:

a) measure the distance round the head;

b) decide on the height of the crown of the hat;

c) decide on the width of the brim of the hat.

To make the pattern

When determining the measurements around the top of the crown and the brim on the pattern, place the tape measure on its edge to measure around the curve.

Do the same for the curved edges on the side of the crown.

Add 1.25 cm ($^1/_2$ in) seam allowance all round.

You will need

Sufficient soft leather to cut out one top of crown, one side of crown, two brims and a strip (which can be joined) to go all around the edge of the brim. (**Note**: You cannot use the cut-out from the brim for the top of the crown as there will be no seam allowance.)

A sewing machine with a leather-point needle.

Strong sewing thread.

Sufficient wide bias binding to fit around the head plus 2.5 cm (1 in).

Leather glue.

Pattern P soft leather hat

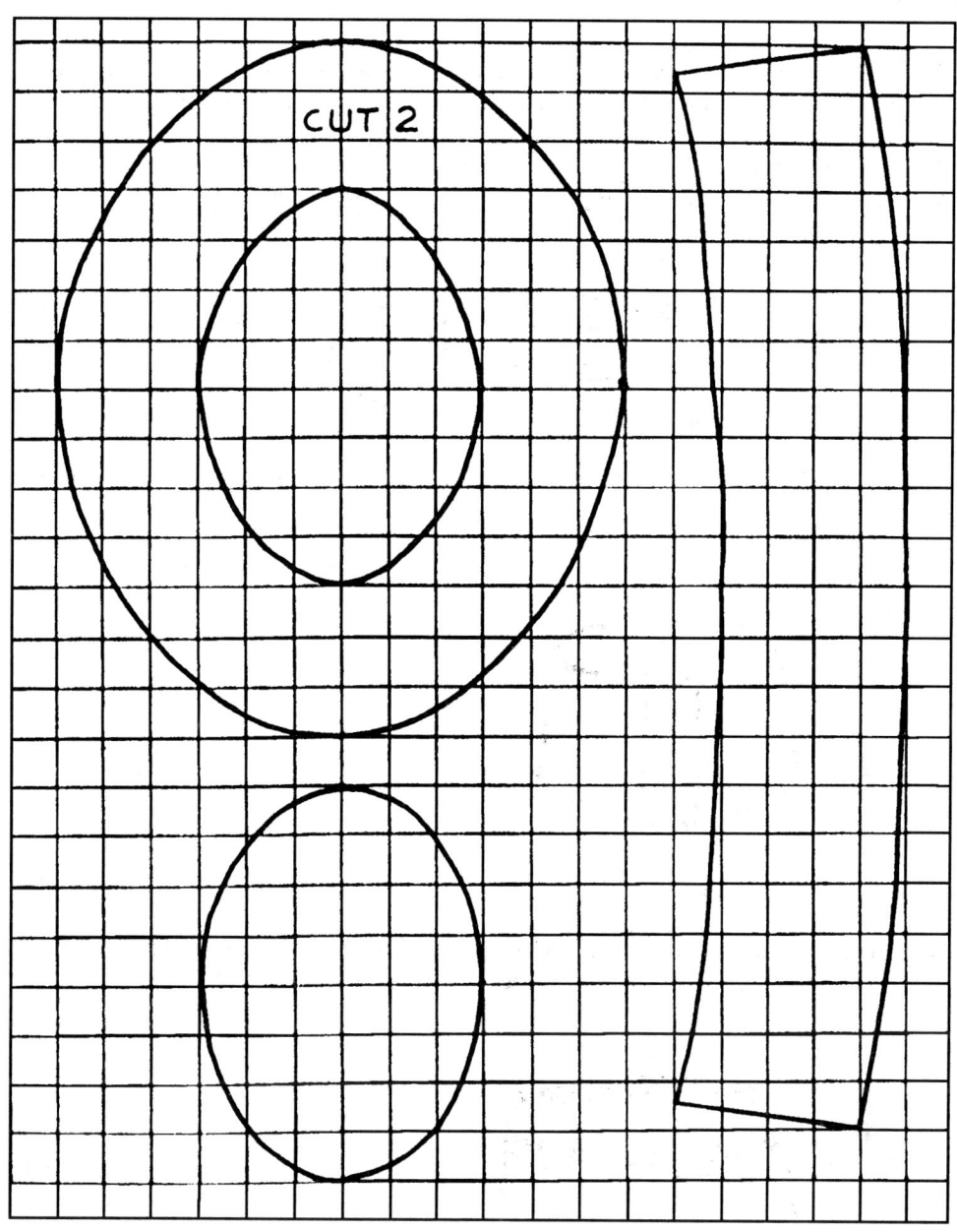

Divide distance round the head by 20 to find the size of each square.

Add 1.25 cm ($\frac{1}{2}$ in) seam allowance all round.

To make

1. Cut out one top of crown, one side of crown, two brims and, if desired, a strip (which can be joined with a flat seam) long enough to go all the way round the edge of the brim.

2. Dampen and stretch upright the inside seam allowance of both brims. Allow to dry (Fig. 95). Alternatively, snip into the seam allowance all the way round the inside of the brims.

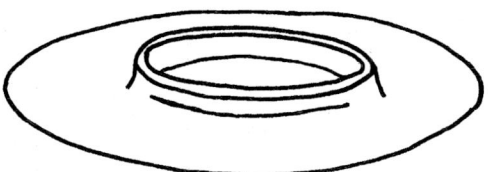

Fig. 95

3. Join the seam in the side of the crown to form a circle, and press the seam flat with a damp cloth and a cool iron (Fig. 96).

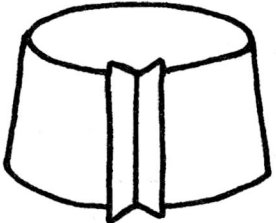

Fig. 96

4. With right sides together, join the top of the crown to the upper edge of the side of the crown. **Note:** This needs care as one piece of leather will try to stretch (Fig. 97).

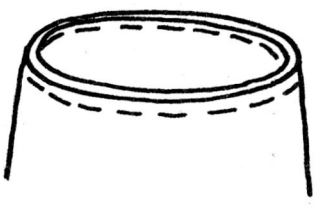

Fig. 97

5. With right sides together, join one brim to the lower edge of the side of the crown. Again, this will need care (Fig. 98).

Fig. 98

6. Trim away the seam allowances around the top and bottom edges of the side of the crown to 0.5 cm ($\frac{1}{4}$ in). Turn through to the right side.

7. Stitch the bias binding to the inside edge of the remaining brim on the right side (Fig. 99).

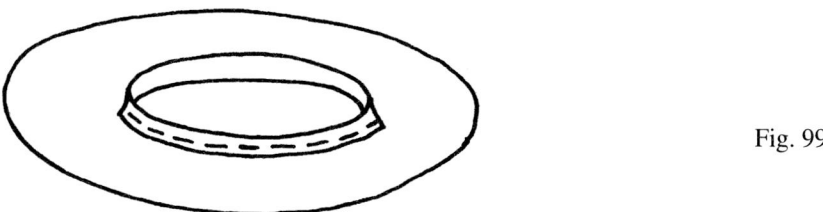

Fig. 99

8. Place the wrong side of one brim to the wrong side of the other brim and stitch together all the way round the outer edge (Fig. 100).

Fig. 100

9. Glue the bias binding up on to the inside of the crown and stitch the edge in place through the side of the crown.

10. From the outside, hand stitch through the seam holding the side of the crown to the brim so that both layers of the brim are held firmly in place.

11. If desired, glue the strip of leather over the edge of the brim, allow to dry and stitch in place through all layers (Fig. 101).

Fig. 101

Optional Extra

Add a band of thin plaited leather or other band of your choice.

Hooded rain cape

You will need

150 cm (50 or 60 in) wide waterproof nylon fabric twice the length of the finished cape plus 15 cm (6 in).

A nylon zip the length of the centre front join without the seam allowance.

24 cm ($9^{1}/_{2}$ in) of 2.5 cm (1 in) wide Velcro.

1 metre (1 yd) cord.

30 cm (12 in) thin elastic.

To make

1. Cut out one back piece and the three front pieces. From the remaining fabric, cut one pair of hood pieces, one pocket, one neck insert and one strip 15 cm (6 in) wide and the same length as the join across the front pieces.

Pattern Q hooded rain cape

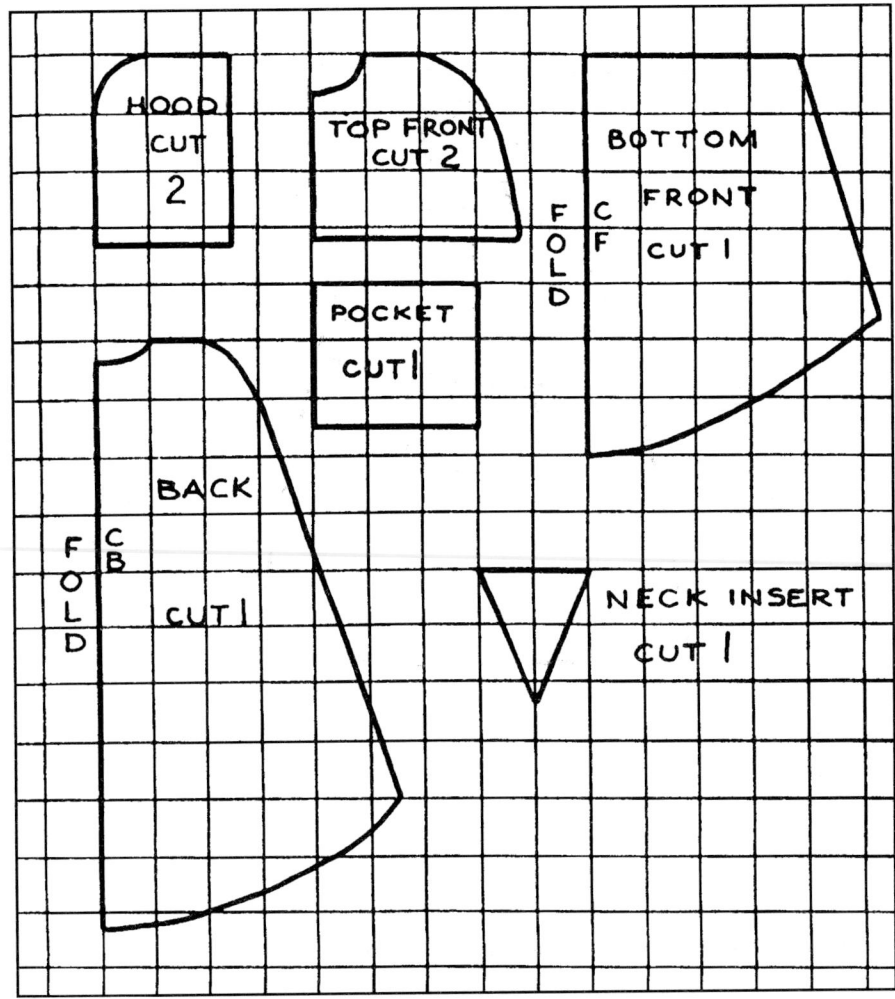

Hold your hands together just above the waist.

Measure across your front from elbow to elbow.

Divide half the distance across from elbow to elbow by 4 to find the width of each column.

Divide the length from the shoulder at the neck edge to the lower hem by 10 to find the height of each row.

Add 1.25 cm ($^1/_2$ in) seam allowance all round.

2. Make a hem along the top edge of the pocket and stitch. Sew the loop strip of Velcro on the right side of the top edge (Fig. 102).

Fig. 102

3. Turn in the remain three edges and sew the pocket on to the lower front piece, twice the seam allowance from the edge (Fig. 103).

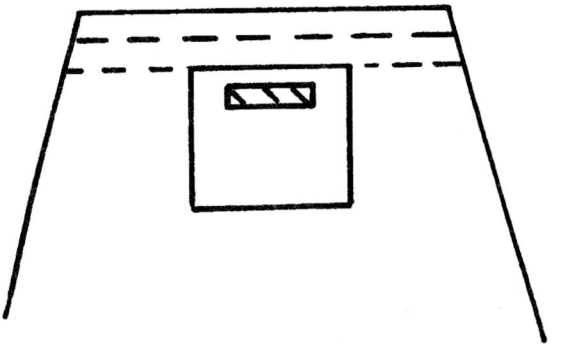

Fig. 103

4. Neaten the top of the neck insert. Insert the zip between the top front pieces and the V, leaving the seam allowances extending above and below the zip. Stitch in place and neaten the edges (Fig. 104).

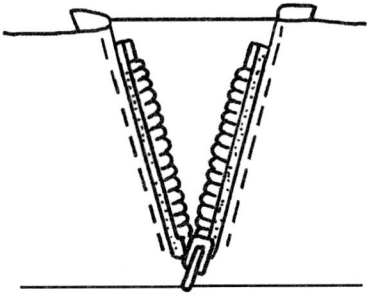

Fig. 104

5. Place the right side of the top front to the right side of the lower front. Fold the long strip in half, wrong sides together, and place it between the two front pieces with raw edges together. Stitch along the seam (Fig. 105). Neaten the seam.

Fig. 105

6. Determine the position of the hook piece of Velcro under the long strip so that it closes the pocket. Stitch in place.

7. Place right side of back to right side of front and join the side seams. Neaten.

8. Join the two halves of the hood together and neaten.

9. Attach the hood to the neck of the cape with the seam allowance around the front edge extending beyond the zip (Fig. 106). Neaten.

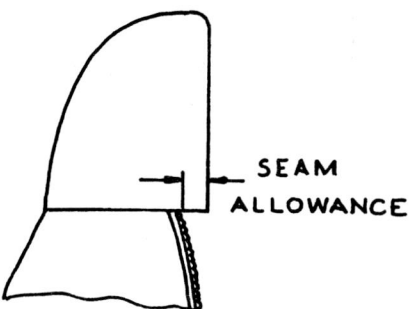

Fig. 106

10. Make a hem around the edge of the hood sufficiently wide to take the cord, and with the edge of the hem level with the edge of the zip (Fig. 107).

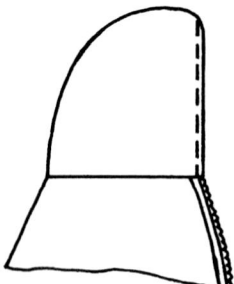

Fig. 107

11. Thread the cord through the hem around the hood and knot both ends.

12. Make a small hem all around the lower edge of the cape.

13. Sew elastic loops to the underside of the front for the wrists at the appropriate position (Fig. 108).

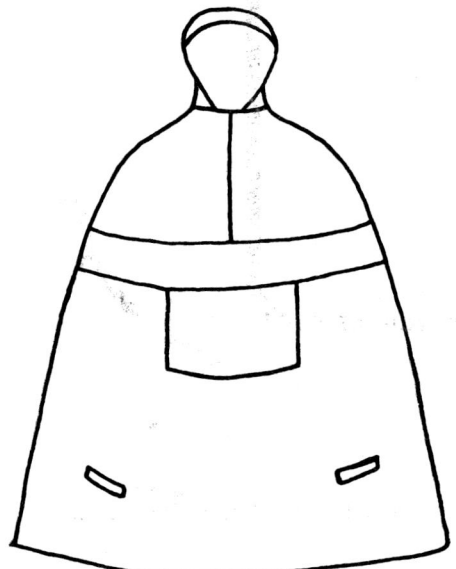

Fig. 108

Optional extra

Sew reflective strips across the back.

Driving apron

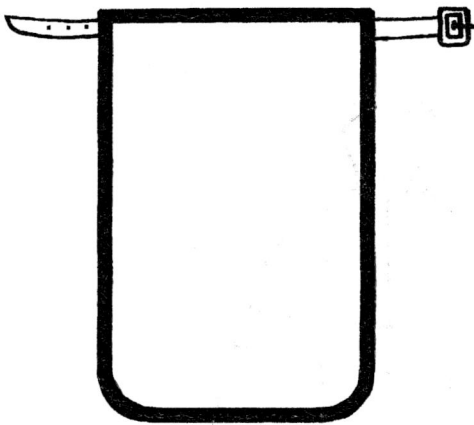

First take the following measurements:

a) the distance from the left back hip bone round the front of the body to the right back hip bone;

b) the distance from the waist to the top of the ankle bone.

You will need

A piece of melton cloth to match the above measurements.

A piece of lining material the same size as the melton cloth, or, for a reversible apron with a waterproof side, a piece of soft leather or leatherette the same size as the melton cloth.

Sufficient 3.75 cm ($1^{1}/_{2}$ in) carpet binding in a matching or contrasting colour.

Sewing thread to match the binding.

Two leather straps long enough to join the apron at the back waist.

A whole roller buckle or other suitable buckle.

To make

1. Cut curved corners to what will be the bottom edge of the apron.

2. Place the lining and melton cloth wrong sides together and stitch together all the way round the edge.

3. Starting at the centre waist, stitch the binding to the edge of the melton cloth side so that approximately one third of the width of the binding protrudes beyond the edge of the work (Fig. 109).

Fig. 109

4. At the corners, fold the binding as shown in Fig. 110 to give a mitred effect. Stitch along the fold from the edge of the binding, up the corner, and back to the edge of the binding again.

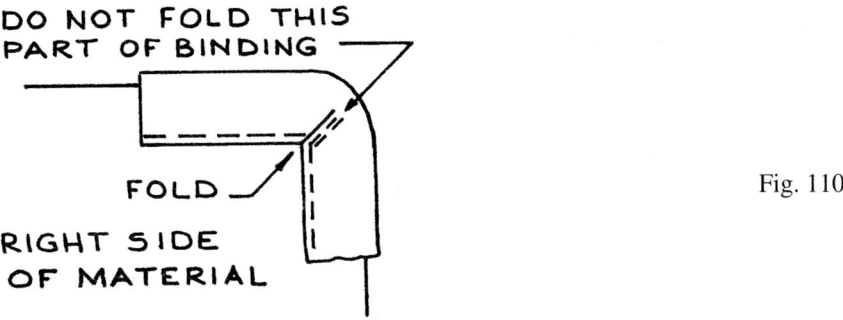

Fig. 110

5. When you reach the place where the binding started, finish off by folding the end of the binding under and stitching across the fold as shown in Fig. 111.

Fig. 111

6. Turn the work over, and fold the binding around the edge of the material. Tack the binding in place on this side and trim off any material which prevents a neat finish. Stitch the binding down so that this row of stitching shows through on the melton cloth side of the work (Fig. 112).

Fig. 112

7. At the corners, fold the binding as shown in Fig. 113 to give a mitred effect.

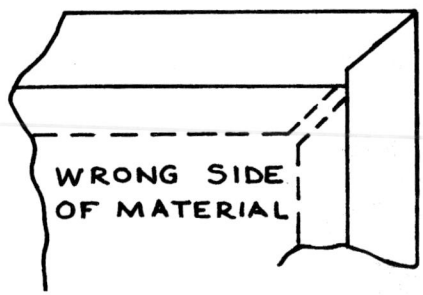

Fig. 113

8. Ease the binding around the curved lower corners.

9. Make holes in one strap. Cut a slot in the other in three stages as shown in Fig. 114 to take the buckle.

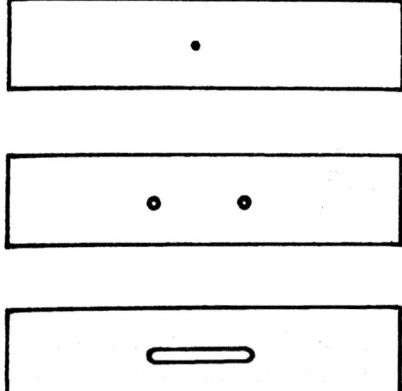

Fig. 114

10. Attach a buckle to the strap (Fig. 115).

Fig. 115

11. Attach this to the left back edge of the top of the apron, and the other strap to the right top edge. Cut the end of the strap with the holes to a point so that it slots easily through the buckle (Fig. 116).

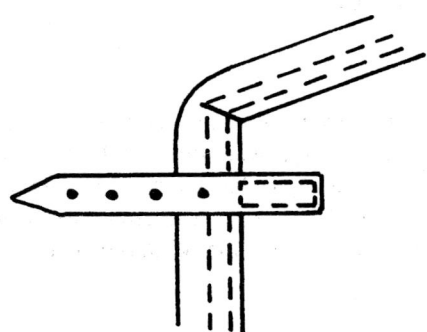

Fig. 116

Side-saddle habit

The jacket is single breasted, waisted and has two back side vents. It is cut away at the front to show the yellow, white or checked waistcoat which is worn under it. There are two buttons at the front and each sleeve also has two buttons. A variety of lapel and collar styles could be used (depending on current fashion and personal preference), so instructions are given for adapting a commercial jacket pattern. The jacket length is such that the skirt/apron does not show below it at the back.

When walking, the lower right edge of the skirt/apron is buttoned up to the back. This edge is attached to the heel of the boot by an elastic loop when mounted.

You will need

A pattern for a single-breasted, waisted jacket to adapt.

Sufficient melton cloth, cavalry twill or other suitable material for the jacket and skirt/apron.

Sufficient lining material for the jacket and skirt/apron.

Interfacing for the jacket.

10 buttons (6 for the jacket and 4 slightly larger ones for the skirt/apron).

30 cm (12 in) of narrow elastic.

Sufficient bias binding to go around the waist of the finished skirt/apron.

The jacket

To cut away the front

1. Cut the corners of the front lower edges as shown in Fig. 117 so that the lower button is approximately 7.5 cm (3 in) above the waist. The top buttonhole should be level with the point of the bust. Cut the front facing to match.

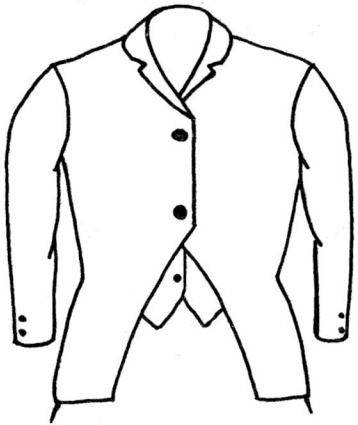

Fig. 117

Other modifications to the pattern

2. Follow the instructions for the showing/hacking jacket starting on page 48 to:

   a) make the jacket wide enough across the back;
   b) make the jacket the correct length;
   c) replace darts with shaping seams;
   d) add side vents to the back;
   e) make a two-piece sleeve from a one-piece sleeve and openings at the cuff;
   f) allow for shoulder pads if necessary.

To make

1. It is essential to keep a hot iron and damp cloth to hand so that you can press each seam as you work.

2. Follow the instructions included with the pattern, but make the additions/alterations necessary as described for the showing/hacking jacket as you get to the appropriate place in the making up as well as including the cut-away front edges.

3. Fasten the front with two buttons and add two buttons to each cuff.

The skirt/apron

Because of its complicated shape, it is advisable to roughly make up the skirt/apron in cotton sheeting first, so that any alterations can be made before cutting out in the expensive main fabric and lining. The seam joining the two pieces together runs from the centre front waist down over the right knee.

The angle at the right knee on the line XY on piece A may need to be adjusted depending on how you sit in the saddle, and the curve of the hem altered to make it horizontal (the hem when the rider is mounted is parallel with the ground with only the left foot and ankle showing beneath it).

To make

1. Cut out one piece A and one piece B in both the main fabric and the lining.

2. Make the darts in the main fabric and the lining of both pieces. On piece B press the waist darts away from the centre back, the hip dart towards the centre back and the knee darts downwards. On piece A press the dart away from the centre front.

3. Cut a strip of main fabric 10 cm (4 in) long by 5 cm (2 in) wide. Fold as shown in Fig. 118 and stitch down its length to close the open edge.

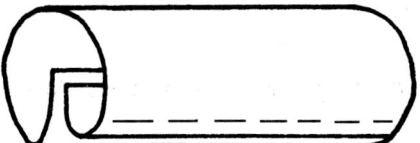

Fig. 118

4. Fold this strip in half and stitch to corner Z on the right side of the main fabric on piece B to make a button loop to fit the larger buttons (Fig. 119).

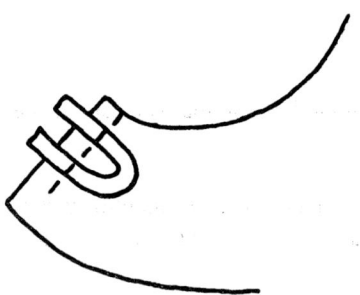

Fig. 119

Pattern R side-saddle skirt/apron piece A

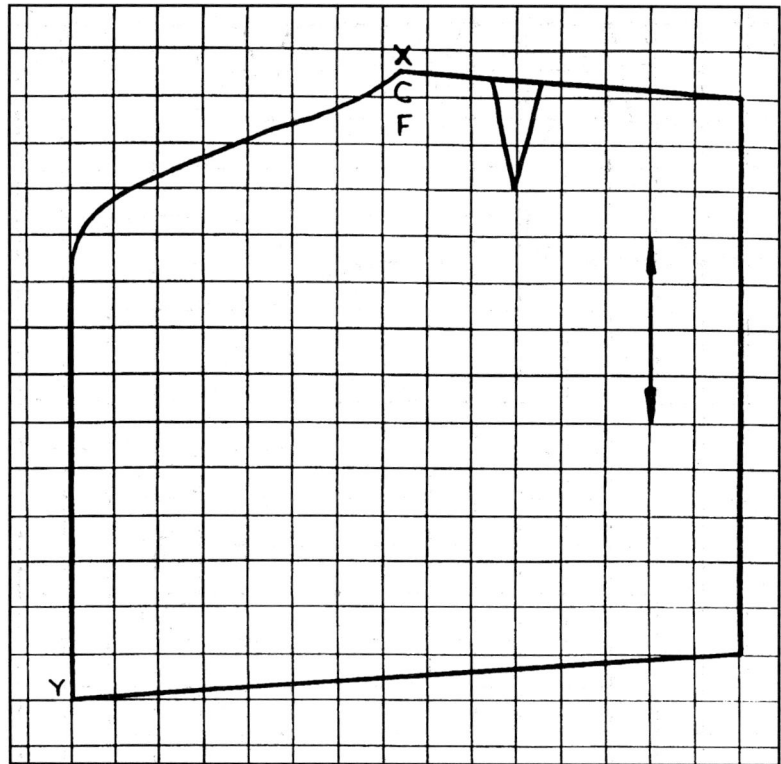

The angle of the line XY may need to be altered depending on how you sit in the saddle, and the curve of the hem might also need to be adjusted to make it parallel with the ground when mounted.

Adjust the length from the waist to the knee by adding to the width of the pattern to increase the measurement, or reducing the width to decrease it.

Divide the waist measurement by 20 to find the width of each column.

Divide the measurement from the waist to just above the ankle by 12 to find the height of each row.

A seam allowance of 1.25 cm ($^1/_2$ in) has been allowed all round.

Pattern S side-saddle skirt/apron piece B

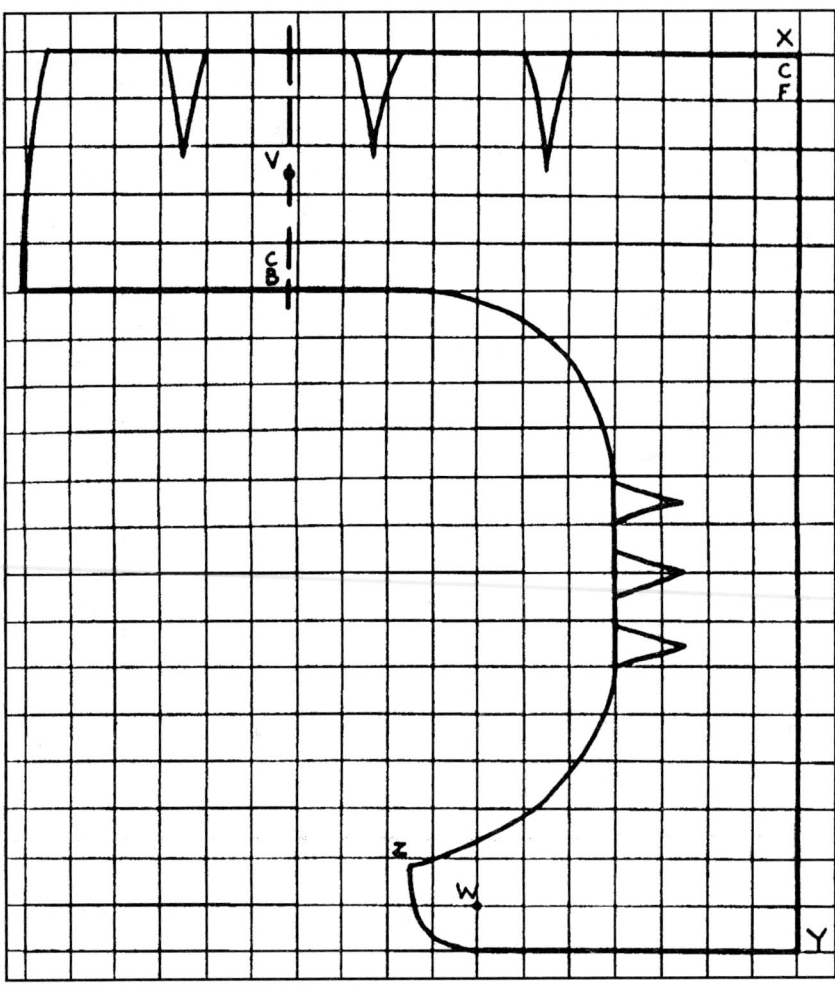

Divide the waist measurement by 20 to find the width of each column.

Divide the measurement along the line XY on pattern piece A by 19 to find the height of each row.

A seam allowance of 1.25 cm ($^1/_2$ in) has been allowed all round.

5. Join the main fabric pieces together along the line XY. Repeat with the lining. Press both seams open.

6. Place the right side of the main fabric to the right side of the lining and stitch together around all sides except the waist. Snip off the corners.

7. Turn through to the right side and press all around the edge, pressing the button loop outwards (Fig. 120).

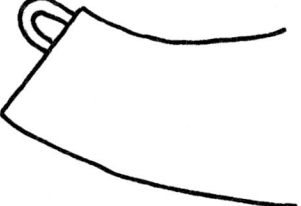

Fig. 120

8. Stitch the lining to the main fabric along the edge of the waist close to the top.

9. Bind the waist with bias binding.

10. Sew three buttons at the left side on piece B, and make corresponding buttonholes on piece A.

11. Sew a button half way down the centre back at point V.

12. Fold the elastic in half to make a loop and attach to the lining side of the right hand lower corner at the position marked W on the pattern.

13. Hand stitch through the seams of the main fabric and lining at the knee to hold them together over the leg.